Contexts of Ageing

Contexts of Ageing

Class, Cohort and Community

Chris Gilleard and Paul Higgs

polity

First published in 2005 by Polity Press

Polity Press
65 Bridge Street
Cambridge CB2 1UR, UK

Polity Press
350 Main Street
Malden, MA 02148, USA

ISBN: 0-7456-2949-0
ISBN: 0-7456-2950-4 (pb)

A catalogue record for this book is available from the British Library.

Typeset in 11 on 13 pt Berling
by SNP Best-set Typesetter Ltd, Hong Kong
Printed and bound in Great Britain by MPG Books Ltd, Bodmin, Cornwall

For further information on Polity, visit our website: www.polity.co.uk

Contents

Preface

Ageing is not what it used to be. As life in the West grows longer and more leisurely, states and individuals are presented with new challenges in organizing the lifecourse. These challenges affect both the beginnings and the ends of adulthood. Old age and the end of 'adulthood' can be viewed from two conceptually distinct perspectives. The first focuses upon ageing as a process or processes of biological change occurring after reproductive maturity has been attained. While it is not clear how determinate these 'ageing processes' are, nor what might need to happen for them to change, biological parameters are no longer treated as the fixed, obdurate features of an unchangeable human nature. A degree of indeterminacy is now recognized (Kirkwood 1999). The choice is whether to map or test its boundaries.

The second perspective concentrates on the social and cultural position that later life and ageing occupy within society. Ageing in this sense is about the social and cultural identity associated with the latter part of the lifecourse. Such identities assume the existence of a socialized lifecourse in which a regular distinction is made between adult and later adult life. The nature of that distinction and the structures that support or undermine it are less stable than the biological parameters governing ageing, varying over time and between societies. The structures that organize and define what later life can be are the principal concerns of this book.

If ageing is more indeterminate than before, the expectation of later life has become more certain. No longer an uncommon, risky and relatively brief period of life before death, later life constitutes an extended and relatively secure arena within the individual lifecourse. It is an arena where 'old age' no longer forms the dominant, unquestioned theme. That is the essence of the cultural turn we highlighted in our earlier book, *Cultures of Ageing* (Gilleard and Higgs 2000). While much about old age has not changed, for people approaching retirement, old age has ceased to be the dominant motif. This evolving swathe of post-working life unconstrained by disability and dependency continues to concern us. We are seeking in this book to examine the contexts that are helping to realize this reformulation of later life and what constraints still exist that hobble and restrain its possibilities. While we are aware that much of the modern lifecourse remains unchanged, our interest is on what is changing – about the nation-state, about work and class, about social relationships and the family. None of these structures have disappeared, nor have ageing and old age. But all of these structures are changing, and with them ageing is changing too. These are the contexts of ageing that we explore in this book.

CJG and PFDH

Acknowledgements

This book develops some of the themes originally outlined in *Cultures of Ageing: Self, Citizen and the Body*. We would like to thank all those who have read, commented upon, and debated our arguments. In particular we would like to thank Scott Bass, Martin Hyde, Ian Jones, Rick Moody, Graham Scambler, John Vincent and Dick Wiggins. The usual caveats apply.

Some of the material in this book has been presented at several conferences held over the past three years, including the International Sociological Association's XV World Congress of Sociology at Brisbane, the 34th European Behavioural and Social Science Research Section of the International Association of Gerontology at Bergen in 2002, the 6th Biennial Conference of the European Sociological Association in Murcia, and the 56th Annual Conference of the Gerontological Society of America in San Diego in 2003. We are grateful for the opportunity to debate and develop our ideas in these fora. We have also benefited from numerous seminar programmes, including those hosted by King's College London, London Medical Sociology Group and University College London. Finally we would like to thank particularly South West London & St. George's Mental Health NHS Trust and the Centre for Behavioural and Social Sciences in Medicine at UCL for giving both of us the time and space to complete this book.

1

Introduction

The flux in the social organization of the 'post-modern' lifecourse has rendered later life an increasingly contested social field. The origins of that contestation lie, we argue, in the dislocations of the relationship between labour and capital, in changes in the bond between the generations, and in transformations in the nature of community. If the industrial revolution of the nineteenth century established the conditions for universal retirement, the cultural developments of the late twentieth century have generated a new set of terms by which the lifecourse can be understood. Working through the implications of this 'cultural revolution' has de-stabilized many of the institutional structures underpinning the 'modern life cycle', at the same time 'disembedding' individuals from refuge in 'community'. The 'third age' is an important pre-cipitate of these changes.

As first outlined by Peter Laslett (1989), the term 'third age' is widely used to describe life after the responsibilities of paid employment and child rearing are over (Rubinstein 2002: 31). It is typically treated as a 'new' period in the lifecourse, neither middle age nor old age, but a kind of hybrid of the two. It is the crown of life, a success of both society and of the individual, equally distanced from the responsibilities of adulthood and the infirmities of old age. Weiss and Bass have summarized the posi-tion of the third age as follows:

> The life phase in which there is no longer employment and childraising to commandeer time, and before morbidity enters to limit activity and mortality brings everything to a close, has been called the Third Age. Those in this phase of life have passed through

a first age of youth, when they prepared for the activities of maturity, and a second age of maturity, when their lives were given to those activities, and have reached a third age in which they can, within fairly wide limits, live their lives as they please, before being overtaken by a fourth age of decline. (Weiss and Bass 2002: 3)

Later Life and the Third Age as a New Social Field

The images and assumptions that working and non-working people have of later life are viewed through the prism of a retirement that has become less homogeneous, less totalizing, and, potentially, less restrictive than it once was. Consequently, the social identities of 'older people' are less easily defined, and the social fields they occupy less easily demarcated. Set against these changed circumstances, periodizing later life as the third age is equally problematic and riven with contradictions. We are not suggesting that later life, as the third age, occupies a newly privileged or particularly valued position within society. Clearly, it does not. Nor by writing about the third age do we mean to imply that there exists a strong sense of collective identity amongst the retired population, either as third agers, senior citizens or old age pensioners. On the contrary, the cultures of the third age create a diffuse and often contradictory set of positions for retired people within society. While retirement is generally treated as a 'social good', something to be sought rather than resisted, there exists uncertainty about how it is to be lived and whether it represents quite the position of agency that is often claimed for it. Even when agency is experienced, there are many who would argue that it amounts to no more than 'false consciousness' masking a dangerous, amoral denial of the realities of disablement, decay and death (pretty much in that order). Those who seek to realize a third age are often accused of either bankrupting the nation, squandering the wealth of future generations, or seeking to overthrow the natural order of things by pursuing misguided fantasies of rejuvenation and facile myths of immortality.

For us, the third age is neither some anti-ageing cure-all nor a set of demographic or biological markers distinguishing those who are ageing successfully from those who are not. The third age is not product, category, or lifestyle. Equally, it cannot be reduced to a particular state of mind. Our argument is that it is better likened to a 'cultural field' realized through the activities and discourse of particular social actors within whose lives it acquires concrete form. But those forms, those representations of the third age, are inevitably ambiguous. It would be a mistake, therefore, to identify the third age too closely with the characteristics of those in whose lives it is realized. The third age is not fundamentally gendered, racialized or reducible to the cultural precipitate of class position or status. It is a cultural field whose boundaries escape the confines of any specific community of interest.

Defining the third age in these cultural terms may appear to ignore contemporary academic approaches that have highlighted the status divisions of gender and ethnicity in later life. While it is possible to focus upon either gender or ethnicity as the prism through which the third age is studied, such perspectives give less prominence to the material and temporal contexts that we believe are actively shaping the social terrain of later life. In *Cultures of Ageing* (Gilleard and Higgs 2000), we acknowledged the inequalities of gender and ethnicity that continue to overshadow the possibilities and opportunities of later life. We would certainly not wish to deny those aspects of contemporary social realities. However, our intention is not primarily to study inequality in later life. The prominence we give to class is because of its significance in establishing the social and structural conditions that shape our ageing societies, rather than because of its role in representing inequality across the lifecourse. This may betray a certain ontology and ordering of processes, but it is not the place to engage with analyses that have these different starting points.[1]

Within the academic community and within society at large, there remains considerable ambivalence toward the nature and reality of the third age, as well as its relevance to 'old age'. Retirement is treated, in the media and in much academic literature, either as a period of marginalized poverty, sustained by state handouts and lacking any separate cultural form, or as a position of wealth and idleness in which the narcissistic, materialist culture of a privileged few is sustained and supported by the labour of the many. Oscillation between these contrasting images of retirement and retired people – as either the 'deserving poor' or the 'idle rich' – reflects the evident inconsistencies of contemporary later life. Some retired people own expensive houses despite low incomes, while others pay rent for poorly maintained properties in impoverished neighbourhoods. Some retired people benefit from generous, well-maintained occupational pension schemes, while others who were once as equally well paid find themselves facing an impoverished retirement after the collapse of their company's pension fund. Some widows benefit significantly from their husbands' pension schemes and life insurance policies; others, facing severe poverty, remain too proud or too ashamed even to seek income support. Some people who have 'aged' in the same neighbourhood throughout their adult lives find themselves isolated and alone in their retirement, strangers in familiar settings, while others who have set out on a new life in a new house in a new country enjoy the benefits of a better climate and a lower cost of living while being part of a new-found community of compatriots. Such are the shifting realities of the third age.

Given the complexities that are attached to the third age, we shall begin by assembling evidence concerning the actual material circumstances of older people in contemporary Western societies. In order for retirement to function as a 'secured' social field for the third age, it is important to demonstrate that there exists sufficient material equivalence in the circumstances of people of retirement age and of those who are actively engaged in the labour market. To establish the temporal distinctiveness of this equivalence, it is necessary also to document the time frame within which these material circumstances have emerged. In the following section of this chapter, we review several key indicators that reflect the material basis from which a more diverse and culturally realizable later life is being fashioned, together with recent trends that illustrate the extent of the transformation of retirement.

We draw our evidence from (mostly Western) Europe and North America. Although the third age can be treated as a 'global' construct, capable of being extended to all corners of the world, as a phenomenon of mass culture it is expressed primarily within the developed world. A global future for the third age is still some way off. Whether and how it might be realized within the existing structure of the world economy is a question requiring a considerably broader analysis than the one that we are proposing. For the moment we must content ourselves with treating the third age as a phenomenon of the 'Westernized' life course, one that has been conceived and delivered against the historical backdrop of modernity.

The Material Realization of the Third Age

In pre-industrial Europe, the opportunity to enjoy retirement was the privilege of a favoured few who, as a reward for loyal service, were guaranteed by their lord or sovereign a life pension. For those who had no need to work in the first place of course, the distinction between work or service and retirement was minimal. A few wealthy people did choose to retire, typically buying themselves into some religious institution, where by paying a fixed sum of money (a prebendary), they could enjoy the privilege of a supported passage into the next life. Occasionally retirement contracts were drawn up, enabling peasant landowners to transfer their estate to kith and kin in exchange for guaranteed support in their old age (Phillipson 2001). But for the majority of the people work was a lifelong obligation that only sickness and infirmity could end. Since a longer life also meant an increasing risk of sickness and disability, the infirm/decrepit aged were an ever-present category amongst the deserving poor, who, in the absence of sufficient family support, would be reduced to begging or soliciting charity.

Consequently, there was little anticipation of a 'planned' retirement. The main concern – societal and personal – was to avoid the risks of immiseration in old age. The fear of becoming unemployable in later life may well have been present amongst working people since the end of feudal society, but as people began to move away from their own communities in search of work, the risk of impoverishment became much more acute. This heightened sense of vulnerability led to the emergence of mutual benefit or friendly societies, institutions through which the new working class tried to establish some kind of provision against sickness and old age. This system of mutual support and financial provision for sickness and old age was extensively developed in England where the transition toward the modern wage economy was most advanced (Baemreither 1889).

Despite the growth in mutual society membership throughout Europe, stopping work in later life was rarely a decision based on financial planning. According to Paul Johnson's analyses of late nineteenth-century censuses in England and Wales, the number of men still working after the age of 65 fell from just under three-quarters (73 per cent) in 1881 to just under two-thirds (65 per cent) in 1891 (Johnson 1994). During a similar period (1870–1900) in the United States, figures suggest that about three-quarters of the male population aged over 65 were still employed or seeking work, while no more than 20 per cent 'enjoyed' some form of retirement (Ransom and Sutch 1986; Carter and Sutch 1996). Although some writers have argued that a significant proportion of working people did enjoy a period of later life without the necessity of labour, it seems clear that most could not.[2] Many spent it in poverty. In 1892, over 20 per cent of the population aged 65 and over in England and Wales were receiving outdoor poor relief; a further 8 per cent were institutionalized (Nield 1898). At the time, poor relief amounted to approximately one-quarter of the average working man's income, which itself was barely enough to provide for more than the everyday necessities of food, clothing and shelter (Thomson 1984). Amongst those able to work, one in five could not be sure of earning enough to stave off 'primary poverty' (Rowntree 1901).

Even after the introduction of state pensions, there was no great increase in the number of people retiring from the labour force. Most pensioners were still counted amongst the poor in the period immediately after the Second World War.[3] Although retirement became a more socially and materially secure position, it was a slow process. Between the end of the war and the 1973 oil crisis, the economic position of retired people changed relatively slowly compared with the rising affluence of the working population. Only when the beneficiaries of the post-war affluence themselves began retiring did pensioners' economic position improve significantly, at the same time as average wage rises began to slow down. The result was a gradual convergence in the average net income of working and retired people.

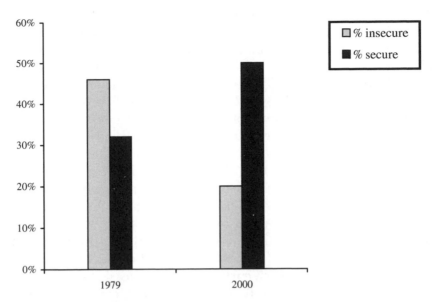

Figure 1.1 Percentage of UK pensioners in positions of financial security and insecurity, 1979–2000. Source: Office for National Statistics, Pensions Analysts Division 2002: tables 17and A17.

In Britain, the proportion of pensioner households in the lowest quintile of the overall net income distribution (which may be taken to represent 'material insecurity') declined, while the proportion with incomes in the top three quintiles (which may be taken to represent 'material security') increased substantially (see fig. 1.1).

This transformation from insecurity to security in later life was not unique to Britain. Compared with other Western countries, the economic position of retired people in Britain is rather worse (Disney and Whitehouse 2001: figs 2.3 and 2.7). In Canada, for example, the median net income of 'retired' couples rose in real terms from Canadian $26K in 1973 to Canadian $38K in 2000, an increase which far exceeded that of people 'of working age'.[4] During the same time period, the proportion of Canadian retirees ranked amongst the poor fell from 28 per cent to 5 per cent (Osberg 2001). In the United States, during the same period, the average income of retired households rose by over 50 per cent, from US $23,382 in 1975 to $35,589 in 2000, while the proportion of pensioner households at or below the poverty line fell from 25 per cent to 16 per cent (US Census Bureau 2003a, 2003b).

In France, between 1970 and 1996 the net income of retired households rose by almost 125 per cent, from F.Fr. 43 K to F.Fr. 96 K, while the net income of households of those still working rose by just over 50 per cent, from F.Fr. 69 K to F.Fr. 105 K. Retired people's standard of living rose by almost 5 per cent per year, whilst that of wage-earners rose by less than 2 per cent per year (Guillemin and Roux 2003: 5–6). In 1970, one in four pensioner households in France was still classified 'poor'; by 1997 that figure had fallen to less than one in twenty. From 1971, when retired people's net household income was less than two-thirds that of working age households (62 per cent), it had grown to a point of near equivalence (91 per cent) by 1996 (Conseil d'Orientation des Retraites 2001: 30–1). By the mid-1990s, German pensioner incomes had increased to 84 per cent of the net median income of the working age population, a level of economic well-being matched by Italian retirees whose median net income was 87 per cent of the national median (Casey and Yamada 2002: 39–40). Between 1973 and 1993 poverty rates amongst West German men and women aged 65 and above virtually halved, falling to below 6 per cent probably for the first time in history (ZUMA 2003a: 6).

A recent OECD report on incomes in retirement across a number of member countries indicates the distance travelled. It concluded:

> In most countries people experience almost no or only a minor reduction in their standard of living when moving from later working life to retirement . . . [whilst social security] systems have been largely successful in preventing very low incomes in old age. (OECD 2001b: 10)

Not only have incomes risen and poverty rates fallen within the retired populations of the developed world during the last two and a half decades, but retirement as a period of life has grown substantially. More people have been taking the opportunity

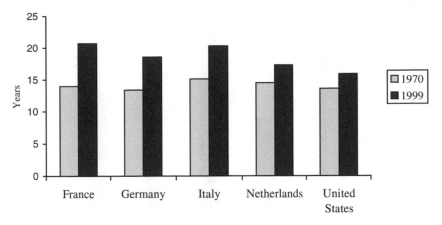

Figure 1.2 Increases in the length of retirement between 1970 and 1999 (selected OECD countries, males). Source: Table V.2, OECD Economic Outlook, no. 72, section V: Increasing employment: the role of later retirement (OECD 2002: 7).

to retire earlier without the fear of impoverishment and with the reasonable expectation of many more years of life. In the Netherlands, median age of male retirement fell from 63.2 in the mid-1970s to 59.9 by the mid-1990s; in West Germany, it fell from 62.3 to 60.3; in Italy from 61.6 to 58.8; in Spain from 64.8 to 61.6; and in Sweden from 64.4 to 63.7. As a result of increased life expectancy and earlier exit from the labour market, the time spent in retirement has risen. Increasingly, the labour of adult life is being exchanged for leisure in later life (see fig. 1.2).

Paralleling the increased material security of retirement has been a rise in consumption during retirement. In the USA, between 1984 and 1999, the overall expenditure of people aged between 65 and 74 grew steadily closer to that of all adults (from 72 per cent to 81 per cent of the average household's expenditure). Expenditure on entertainment has risen even more dramatically, from 56 per cent to 83 per cent of average adult expenditure.[5] A similar change has taken place in Europe. Expenditure on 'leisure goods' by those aged 65–74 in Britain has risen from 53 per cent to 72 per cent of that of the average family household (Department of Employment 1986: 58; Office of

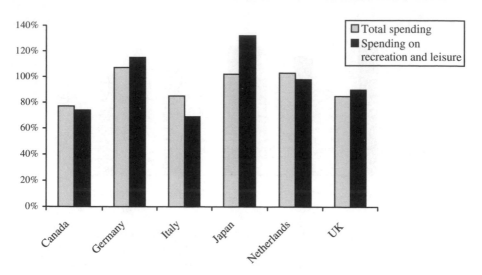

Figure 1.3   Retired couples' consumption as a percentage of that of working couples in six OECD countries, 1998–9. Source: Casey and Yamada 2002: 39.

National Statistics 2002a: 36). By the end of the 1990s, the net consumer expenditure of retired couples frequently matched – and in some countries exceeded – that of couples who were still working (see fig. 1.3).

Reflecting these rising levels of expenditure has been a steady growth in ownership of key 'black' and 'white' domestic goods amongst retired person households. Between the two World Wars the electrification of domestic households increased, and by the outbreak of the Second World War the majority of households across North America and Europe were connected to national electricity supply systems. Although this provided the necessary conditions for the purchase and use of such new household electrical goods as refrigerators, cookers, washing machines, irons, radios, telephones and, later on, TVs and record players, ownership of black and white electrical goods was largely restricted to middle-class households until the late 1950s (Bowden and Offner 1996; Reagin 1998). Between 1950 and 1975, there was a steady growth in the number of ordinary households owning these goods.

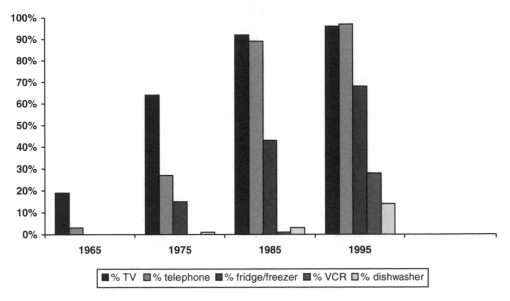

Figure 1.4 Growth in ownership of durable electrical goods in West German pensioner households, 1965–95. Source: ZUMA 2003b: 7, 12, 17, 22.

Even then, such signs of affluence were slower to reach the households of retired people. The gradual consumer 'catch-up' by retired households took place later, during the 1980s and 1990s as these figures from West Germany illustrate (see fig. 1.4).

Similar patterns of 'catch-up' were evident in Britain. Between 1975 and 2000, telephone ownership amongst pensioner households grew from 38 per cent to 97 per cent, and ownership of fridge/freezers from 21 per cent to 92 per cent. In 1975 few households owned either a video cassette recorder (VCR) or a personal computer (PC), but by 2001, 77 per cent of pensioner households had their own VCR and 20 per cent their own home PC. Even more remarkable is the growth in mobile phone ownership: by 2001, almost two-thirds of men and women aged 60–74 had a mobile phone.[6]

At the end of the twentieth century, people had more income in retirement, more time to spend it in, and a wider variety of material resources through which they could enjoy it. The capital that they were bringing to retirement had also grown. This applies firstly to their pension wealth, if one includes in addition to any personal or occupational pension fund wealth, the notional wealth represented by the social security/pension payments they can anticipate receiving over the course of their (anticipated) retirement (Hobson 1999: 1163–4). While 'ownership' of 'pension wealth' is inherently problematic, as we shall see in later chapters, the significance of this increase cannot be understated. The massive and continuing growth of pension funds world-wide (most evident in Australia, Britain, Canada, the Netherlands, New Zealand and the United States) attests to this rising source of wealth (Blackburn 2002: 6). As more and more countries seek to establish a second or third 'privatized' pillar to offset the rising costs of state social security payments, the significance of 'portable' pension wealth will come to dominate the world's economies, increasing the problems concerning the ownership of and responsibility for 'retirement'. Inevitably this will make only more problematic the nature of the third age.

For many people in the UK and the USA the asset value of their home exceeds the value of their notional pension wealth and all their other financial assets. Increasing home ownership coupled with growth in the value of domestic housing is playing a significant part in democratizing retirement wealth. In the USA, home ownership amongst those aged 65 and over has risen from around 60 per cent in the early 1960s to over 80 per cent by 2000. For retired couples, it is estimated to be over 92 per cent (US Census Bureau 2002: table 15). Home ownership in Britain has increased from 52 per cent in 1972 to over 80 per cent in 2001 (for two-person pensioner households) although it is still less than 60 per cent for single pensioners (ONS 2003: table 4.6; OPCS 1975b: table 1.10). In France, there has been a similar increase in home ownership amongst older couples, rising from just under 55 per cent in 1972 to over 77 per cent in 1995 (OPCS 1975b: table 2.69; Whitten and Kailis 1999: table 3). OECD research confirms this high and increasing level of home ownership amongst older people, in most Western countries. This, they believe, will help level the playing field between rich and poor retirees, since 'in most countries . . . some 70 per cent or more of older couples *in the lowest income quintile* still have housing wealth' (OECD

2001b: 42–4). Excluding notional pension wealth, except for the very richest, housing accounts for the largest element of the total wealth of retirees across most countries (OECD 2001b: 43). Although the wealth contained in one's home is not easily realizable, increased home ownership in later life has some very direct effects upon the standard of living in later life. In Britain, housing constitutes the single largest item of expenditure amongst working age households (primarily through rents and/or mortgage repayments). For retired households, in contrast, both food and drink, and travel and leisure, exceed their housing costs (ONS 2002a: 36 and 110–11).

Retired people possess more wealth than people of working age. Based on Inland Revenue figures of identified personal wealth for 2000/1, those aged 65 and over held over 27 per cent of the UK's net personal wealth, although they constitute only 15 per cent of its population.[7] This pattern of relatively smaller incomes, reduced outgoings, but increased wealth is common amongst retired people in the affluent nations. Whilst the lifetime accumulation of wealth has been evident historically, it was confined primarily to the elite wealth-owning class in society. Now it is becoming a trend that describes the circumstances of the majority of older people.[8] Moreover, older people are retaining more of their retirement wealth throughout their post-working lives, rather than 'spending down' their wealth as they grow older (Bateman, Kingston and Piggott 2001: 43–4). Recent US estimates of trends in wealth indicate that this increase in the wealth of retired Americans looks set to continue (Keister 2000: 134–64). The impact this may have on inter-generational relationships will be addressed in a later chapter.

In addition to increased material wealth, successive cohorts of retirees have begun to accumulate significant human capital, in the form of health and education. The rise of education throughout the twentieth century has meant that the proportion of people entering the work-force with further and/or higher education has steadily risen. Those now leaving work are doing so with better educational qualifications and more years of schooling than any previous cohort of retirees (see fig. 1.5).

Rates of enrolment in higher education tend to be greater in the United States than elsewhere. But what is starkly evident in the US data is equally, though less dramatically, true in Europe.

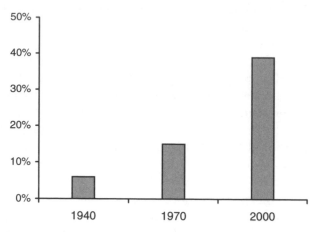

Figure 1.5   Percentage of US population aged 55 and over with some college education, 1940–2000. Source: Table A-1, Education and Social Stratification Branch, US Census Bureau 2003c: A-10–A-13, Internet release date: 21 March 2003.

The proportion of people retiring who have little or no schooling has declined in Italy from 89 per cent in 1950 to 47 per cent in 2000. In France, the number of people aged 60–4 with some college education has risen from 2 per cent to 13 per cent, while in Britain the proportion of those with some tertiary education amongst the present 60–4-year-old population is 29 per cent, compared with less than 4 per cent in 1951.[9] In Sweden, there has been a similar rise in 'well-educated' retirees, with 12 per cent of those reaching retirement in 2005 having completed a college education, compared with less than 8 per cent in 1970. The impact of education on later life is complex, but it certainly seems to contribute to a wider participation in cultural life. This is illustrated by the growth in cultural participation by American men and women in their sixties and seventies over the period 1982 to 1997 (see fig. 1.6 below).

   Those retiring now are not only richer, better educated and more culturally active, but they are also fitter than previous cohorts of retirees. Partly, of course, this is the result of people retiring at younger ages than before. But even when matched for

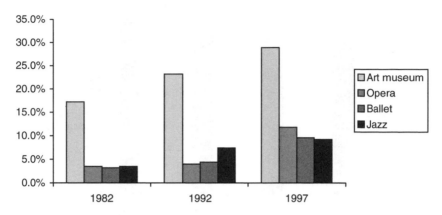

Figure 1.6　Attendance rates at arts events of US men and women aged 55–74, 1982–97. Source: National Endowment for the Arts 1999: table 2; 1994: tables 1 and 2.

chronological age, the proportion of people aged 65 and over reporting some degree of disability or restriction has declined. This is especially clear in the case of the retired population in the USA, where documentation of disability levels going back to the start of the twentieth century indicates a very sizeable increase in the age of onset of various late life chronic illnesses (Fogel 2003). Statistics collected between 1982 and 1999 show that there has been a continuing decline in the numbers of people with a serious disability, defined as limiting the activities of daily living, and a sizeable increase in the number of older people without any disability (see fig. 1.7). European data on disability levels show similar trends toward declining disability rates. Summarizing these studies, Waidmann and Manton conclude 'that, in many countries, there have recently been moderate to large declines in chronic disability in the elderly' (Waidmann and Manton 2000: 38).

In short, there is consistent evidence that, over the last few decades of the twentieth century, there has been a continuing and consistent improvement in the economic, educational and health status of retired people in the developed world. Retired people now constitute a larger section of the population, and retirement occupies a more substantial position within the lifecourse. In these

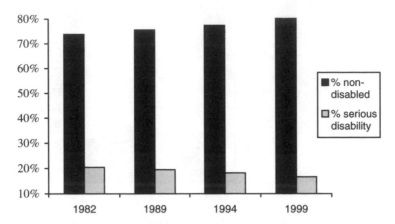

Figure 1.7 Percentage of US 65+ population with no disability and those with a serious (ADL) disability. Source: Manton and Gu 2001: table 1.

ageing societies, later life has become healthier, wealthier and wiser. More income and income from more diverse sources, together with higher levels of educational achievement and home ownership, all add up to improved well-being (see A. E. Barrett 2003; Krueger et al. 2003; Robert and House 1996). While none of these indicators represent the third age *per se*, they do represent some of the key material conditions that facilitate access to the cultural field of the third age.

Contextualizing the Third Age: Terms of Engagement

Having described the material progress toward establishing a third age, we now consider the factors contributing to its social and cultural realization, by which we mean how the third age is practised and given meaning within the lives of retired people. What are the opportunities and constraints that exist for such individuals that encourage or discourage participation in a third age? What factors determine the terms and conditions underlying an individual's engagement with a third age? And, finally, what are the processes that threaten to close down the third age, collectively and individually, and replace it with a downsized old age?

The third age, we argue, exists as both a social and a cultural phenomenon. It is social in so far as it rests upon certain social practices in order for its existence to be realized. The key institutional structure here is retirement. It is cultural in so far as it is given symbolic meaning through social discourse and lifestyle practices. Within this sphere, the media and socially mediated consumption dominate. What you do after you stop working is retirement. Retirement as an institution is sustained through collective social practices, defined and revised both through social policies and through individual and collective contractual agreements. All of this is set against a background of evolving financial markets. What kind of retirement a person actually has depends upon the individual's participation in cultural spheres beyond those of work and home. More and more, cultural spheres are constituted through forms of consumption rather than through occupation and domestic circumstance.

The third age has been established on the basis of a materially secure retirement, realized through the participation of an increasing number of social actors occupying diverse identities and statuses, across widening social spaces. The primary structures that serve to contextualize later life and frame the boundaries of the third age that are the subject of this book are those of class, cohort and community. We have chosen class because it was class society that gave form to the institution of mass retirement, securing later life from the necessity of labour. Changes in the nature of the economy, and accompanying changes in social (class) relationships continue to influence the position of people before and after retirement. The individual's position within retirement remains structurally attached to his or her past social relations with the productive forces of the economy. Though structurally attached, that position is not overdetermined by that relationship. Changes to labour, capital and the global economy confound the historical link between work and retirement.

Cohort was selected because of the importance of time in the social nature of later life. It is within the lives of particular cohorts born during the twentieth century that the third age has emerged as a period of 'guaranteed' leisure. As successive birth cohorts entered and left the work-force, their participation in the 'productive' economy changed it, as it changed them. As the balance between home and work, labour and leisure, production and consumption, has changed, members of each cohort have had to construct and re-construct the nature and roots of their identities. As life has lengthened, individuals have had to address the challenges of extending their identity outside the boundaries of working life. Consumption has been a key element in facilitating this process.

We focus on community because it is through community that most social and cultural identities are realized. Transformations in the nature of community create and reflect changes in people's identities as well as affecting the nature of identity. Modern life has always threatened to 'disembed' the individual from his or her social world. It has accepted and at times encouraged communities to have limited life expectancies, allowing them to grow, thrive and eventually become irrelevant. Late modernity has seen a blossoming of alternatives to the community of place. These alternative communities privilege sources of identity other than those given by ties of work and family. In a post-work world, such alternative communities provide options for new identities and a new sense of belonging at the same time as demanding new choices, the outcomes of which represent new risks.

Class, Cohort and Community

Class, cohort and community represent elements of structure, making participation in the third age a matter of contingency, at the same time shaping the consciousness through which such engagement takes place. They are also terms that have competing interpretations in the social sciences. To analyse their role in shaping later life and determining the boundaries of the field that is the third age, we must define our use of these terms in this book. We also need to acknowledge their own historical evolution both recognizing that ageing and the contexts of ageing are equally sensitive to change. If the third age is to be more than simply a fashionable form of discourse by which to label later life, it is important to demonstrate that its emergence depends upon

wider processes operating within society that exercise a continuing historical influence on the way in which lives are lived and
understood.

Class analysis has been one of the most enduring elements of
social science and social theory since the time of Marx. There is
a temptation to situate the third age neatly and comfortably
within a class analysis. In this scenario, the struggle of the working
class to gain greater access to resources is played out in the politics of pension reform, the third age representing a secure middle-
class retirement that still eludes the working class. Viewed in this
light, the establishment of mass retirement can be seen as either
an achievement of class struggle, a victory that has enabled the
working class to gain a social good previously restricted to the
bourgeoisie, or as a means of continuing to subdue and contain
the working class by rendering them dependent, a reserve army
of labour. Whatever interpretation one follows, the assumption is
that class struggle lies at the heart of the third age.

But the positions that are struggled for, the resources that are
distributed and redistributed, and the very nature of the surplus
that is created within the economy, do not remain unchanged.
Explanations of social and cultural change, including those of later
life, require additional structures to make them complete. Studies
of cultural change have long emphasized the importance of generations in accounting for the decline of certain cultural forms and
the emergence or re-emergence of others. All individuals change
their habits over time, and learn to treat aspects of the social world
differently at different points in their own lifecourse. New ideas,
new meanings and new practices spread more easily among generations whose lives have been dislocated from existing social and
cultural communities.

Various writers have tried to develop a coherent approach to
using the term 'generation' as a structure through which to understand social change. Despite its ambiguities, it is frequently used,
and increasingly juxtaposed with class as an alternative source of
social and cultural identity. Notions of generational inequality and
inter-generational conflict have been expounded, suggesting that
generation should replace class as the key site of future social conflict (Turner 1998). In this argument, the third age is treated as a
'social good' enjoyed by those now retiring, but one which incurs

a level of debt that can only be repaid through the future exploitation of generations to come. Following on from this, the third age can be represented as a cohort phenomenon – *nouveau riche* retirees determined to hold on to their new-found wealth and content to live off the labours of later generations.

Finally, the third age can be seen as a form of community, a community of identity based upon a set of shared interests and occupying a common cultural space. These communities may be physically located, such as the retirement communities in Arizona or those on the Spanish Costa Brava. They may be politically driven, creating constituencies like the pensioner parties or the Gray Panthers. Alternatively, they may be new tribes 'characterised by fluidity, occasional gatherings and dispersal' (Maffesoli 1996: 76), like the Recreational Vehicle communities of North America, or the Snowflake communities of Australia's Gold Coast. The third age may be represented by these new communities whose members seek to replace the communities of their past with new identities which affirm a new stage of life.

Class, cohort and community can each lay claim to represent the overdetermining structure of the third age. Our aim is to use these terms as instruments to map its social and cultural terrain. Just as individual characteristics and personal attributes do not constitute the third age, neither do pre-existing social structures. But without reference to individual lives, and without regard to social structures, the third age will remain little more than an irrelevant post-modern fantasy confined to the academy and marketing departments. Although we recognize its liberatory potential, we are also aware of its capacity to be deployed oppressively. As a valid aspiration for the mass of the population, it can be a condition for diversity rather than difference, for opportunity rather than for inequality. But it remains an aspect of contemporary ageing that is easily misunderstood, one that is seen by some as heralding social meltdown.[10] Our book is an attempt to provide a more positive assessment of the third age. To do this successfully necessitates linking the disparate dimensions of the ageing experience within a wider social context. While these dimensions can seem to be confusing and contradictory, nevertheless we believe that a coherent discourse concerning later life can be derived from the outcomes of a more reflexive modernity.

2

Class, Modernity and the Lifecourse

For the last 200 years class has been one of the main sources of social differentiation in Western society (other principle sources of differentiation being gender, urbanization and, in the latter half of the twentieth century, ethnicity). The contemporary conceptualization of class, if not the social reality to which it refers, emerged during the late eighteenth and early nineteenth centuries. In the political and philosophical writings of the time, 'class' usurped 'rank' or 'status' as the preferred term to describe the basic social structure that determined how people were treated by their fellows and how they in turn treated others. The language of class served to articulate as well as reflect the consciousness that new social divisions were being thrown up by the rapid industrialization and urbanization of early nineteenth-century society that seemed unrelated to the distinctions governing the 'old' society of land, locality and nobility.

These early writings treated class as a novel phenomenon arising from the organization of a nation's economy. The establishment of the firm created a division between those whose income derives from their labour for the firm and those who derive their wealth from employing and directing that labour. This division of society was not infrequently treated as simply the distinction between rich and poor, with the urban poor having no alternative means for ensuring their social reproduction beyond selling their labour. Historians of the period have debated whether nineteenth-century society was adequately and accurately represented by this simple binary opposition of capital and labour, but at the time this division was a key point of tension in a rapidly changing, rapidly expanding society. Gradually, 'class' discourse became articulated in the policies of the time shaping the way that local and national governments addressed poverty and the various groups that constituted the poor.

It was within the context of this polarized society that retirement emerged as a political issue. Groups close to the state such as senior members of the military and the civil service had for some time benefited from official pension arrangements connected to their personal rank and status. Proposals to secure later life against the risk of indigence were first articulated in the eighteenth century, triggered by the need to develop collective forms of social protection amongst the newly formed working classes. As the state was confronted by the need to incorporate the working class into its structures, it too began to formulate a new role for itself in the organization and management of social protection, including that of old age. In this sense, retirement and modern class society share a common point of origin.

The present chapter relates the development of class to changing social relations. Retirement can best be understood within this context. Class politics formed one of the dominant motifs of modernity. Conflicts between the interests of labour and the interests of capital were at the heart of many of the social changes that took place during the late nineteenth and early part of the twentieth century. As the population became urbanized, dependence upon wage labour increased. Older people faced increasing difficulties in competing in this new labour market. Many of those with families who were earning reasonable wages were protected in their old age. Those without such family support, or who lived with low-wage families, faced a growing risk of indigence. In the USA, the Civil War veterans' pension helped alleviate some of these risks, but in Europe, only the Poor Law stood between old age and a pauper's grave. Old age pensions and universal retirement emerged in response to these new circumstances.

After the massive economic and political crises that followed the First World War, the emergence and consolidation of the post-Second World War welfare state can be seen as an attempt to finally stabilize the economic and social relations of capitalism. For T. H. Marshall, the welfare state and its provisions represented the culmination of social rights and the emergence of social equality (Marshall 1992). His would remain the established view across most Western societies for the next thirty years. The post-war political and institutional consensus was that the working class had been effectively incorporated as an equal partner with business and government in the management of the economy and the development of social policy. Universal retirement was achieved throughout most of Europe and the industrialized world as part of this social compact. The precise conditions under which retirement could be enjoyed reflected both social policy goals as well as individual work histories. For the majority of countries retirement income was linked to earnings-related contributions. Even in countries such as Denmark, New Zealand and the UK, where it was financed largely as a flat-rate benefit through general taxation, retirement income continued to reflect individuals' notional work-based contributions. Still, the immediate effect of most retirement systems was, to use Esping-Andersen's term, the *decommodification* of later life. By this, Esping-Andersen (1990) meant that later life could be supported independently from participation in the labour market.[1] Although full de-commodification of the lifecourse was never achieved, the implication was that the retired could be removed from the social relations of exploitation, to form a 'déclassé', free-floating stratum within society, maintained on a social wage that lifted them out of the residuum.

This social democratic consensus began to unravel in the mid-Seventies as economic recession compromised the ability of governments to meet their obligations to both capital and labour (Mishra 1984). The corporatist approach to social policy began to break down. The solution began to be seen as the problem. While most attention has focused on the political aspects of this process, it is important to recognize the change in the social structure that underpinned this corporatist solution (Middlemas 1979). The number of people employed in manufacturing industry peaked in the USA and UK during the 1960s. As educational opportunities increased and sectoral shifts in employment led to a changing occupational map, the structural background supporting class identity began to fragment, reducing the potential political solidarity of class. Traditional working-class culture was already in decline (Hobsbawm 1989). If the Sixties represented the first real break in the solidarity of twentieth-century working-class culture, the economic difficulties of the Seventies saw the decline in its structural underpinning. By the Eighties a more profound and thoroughgoing transformation of class society was evident. Paradoxically, the position of retired people was now better than ever before. In the optimistic days of the 1950s Europe's pensioners still seemed to be living under the shadow of the workhouse. By the 1980s, many retired people were finding themselves in a position financially comparable to that of people of working age. Lone parents had taken over as the new poor. The retired population had acquired a spending capacity that was growing closer to that of the rest of the population (Levy 1987; Preston 1984; Thomson 1989).

The welfare society of the post-war era was undergoing a transformation. A new social logic emerged, predicated upon economic neo-liberalism and heightened individualization. Increasing reference was made to the 'post-modernization' of social and cultural relations. Class, it was argued, was no longer a relevant form of social analysis (Pakulski and Waters 1996). Instead of the 'fixed' positions of class society, the new affluence allowed for the construction of 'lifestyle' choices within a society dominated by the mass culture of consumerism (Kammen 2000). What was now stressed was the choice inherent in modern social relations. The rejection of Keynesian macro-economics in favour of reduced public spending and market discipline meant that individual interest was more important than social benefit. The solidarity of the post-war world was undermined by increased individual affluence. This was as true for later life as it was for the newly affluent 'core' workers of the UK, who returned no fewer than four Conservative governments from 1979 to 1992.

Those retiring during the 1980s and 1990s benefited from a series of relative economic advantages that were not shared by those of working age. The growth of occupational pensions and relatively stable work histories during the long post-war 'boom' meant that the recipients of index-linked pensions sustained a better standard of living at the same time as the rise in property values and property ownership increased retirees' assets. That this situation may be both conditioned by and constitutive of the transition from what has been described as 'organized' to 'disorganized' capitalism is not only our starting point; it is central to our thesis. Understanding the current direction of later life depends upon an adequate analysis of changes in the nature of social organization and production within the course of modernity. The distinctions made by writers as diverse as Bauman, Beck, Giddens, Jameson and Lash have major implications for understanding the present and future relationship between work and retirement. The rest of this chapter will seek to explicate this transformation, setting the context for our subsequent exploration of the 'class' position of people in retirement associated with 'Modernity 1' and 'Modernity 2' (Beck, Bonss and Lau 2003).

Organized Versus Disorganized Capitalism

The analysis of class as social stratification or occupational grouping can be contrasted with its analysis as the precipitate of the underlying structure of economic relations. While the former was once capable of being more or less directly mapped on to the latter, class has become less structured and less structuring. This transformation in the dual nature of class – as social structure and as social identity – has arisen as a result of changes in the underlying economic system. As Jameson and many others have pointed out, the stable identities that were created by industrial capitalism have been fragmented by cultural logics of differentiation and hyper-commodification connected with the all-embracing consumerism of an expanding capitalism (Harvey 1989; Jameson 1984; Smith 2000). Understanding the nature of 'post-modernized' capitalism, rather than endlessly looking to revise the occupational stratification of society, forms the necessary preamble to understanding the fragmentation and de-institutionalization of the lifecourse and thereby the changed nature of later life (Erickson and Goldthorpe 1993; Wright 1997).

One of the most significant developments in the late twentieth century has been the transformation in the economies of the affluent nations. Where once national capital dominated the organization of the productive forces and the nation-state provided support, security and governance to both capital and labour, both have become encircled by the operation of a global market. This transformation, from national to global markets, has been accompanied by a number of other changes: from an economy dominated by the industrial sector to one interlaced by extensive and interrelated service sectors; a shift from 'fordism' to 'post-fordism' as the over-riding organizational principle of work across many sectors of the economy; from a more muted mixed economy to one that turns to outsourcing and privatization; and from a closely regulated national financial sector to volatile global financial markets.

While many different terms have been used to describe these changes, it is generally agreed that the form of capitalism that now dominates is notably different from that which existed through-out most of the twentieth century. Lash and Urry (1987) have described this new form as 'disorganized capitalism'. According to these authors, disorganized capitalism differs from 'organized capitalism' in that the impact of the world market not only creates flexible forms of work organization but also breaks down neo-corporatist relations between state and labour and encourages the development of cultural fragmentation. They write:

> Economic change, most notably in the effects on occupational structure connected with the accumulation of capital is subse-quently the precondition of *disorganization* of civil society. The latter, most visible in multiplication and fragmentation of interest groups – inside and outside of the labour movement – is itself the precondition of disorganization in the state, in the ideal typical model. Instantiated in, for example, the decline of neo-corporatism, the development of the catch-all party, and class dealignment. (Lash and Urry 1987: 7)

These differences between forms of regulation and forms of control have had an impact on the nature of social class, especially in relation to the way that work is undertaken and by whom.[2] While some of Lash and Urry's arguments relating to core and periphery work-forces are no doubt exaggerated, the changing nature of how individuals fit into the work-force bears closer examination.

The single-career work history, the idea of the 'family wage', and the gendered division of labour have all become problematic. Even the distinction between what constitutes full- and part-time work has become open to challenge as greater emphasis is placed upon work-force flexibility. Distinctions between white- and blue-collar jobs have become blurred, whilst the expansion of further and higher education has confounded the role of educational qualifications in reproducing the divisions of class. Work is increasingly subject to time-limited contracts, and outcomes are built into job descriptions. Working life has become both more conditional and more individualized as the idea of a standardized working life has lost its centrality as the principle organizing structure for the lifecourse. Still, there is much continuity, and most people's working lives are not scarred by periods of unemployment. Some have argued that jobs rather than work itself have become more flexible and less stable. The point to note, however, is that the stability that was taken for granted in the past now has to be fought over if it is to be maintained. These and other related changes have led some to conclude that a new form of modernity (if not a post-modernity) has emerged that is gradually de-institutionalizing what once passed as the modern lifecourse.

Routes to Modernity 2

Ulrich Beck and his colleagues have argued that the shift toward disorganized capitalism is more than a transition in the ordering and organization of capitalism. Developing the idea of 'reflexive modernization', they claim that a second modernity has emerged out of the first modernity that was associated with industrialization and the rise of the nation-state. A key facet of those first modern societies was that they were organized on the basis of 'full employment'. What Beck and his colleagues mean by this is that

> status, consumption and social security all flow from participation in the economy, according to a model first propounded in the eighteenth century and finally realized in the twentieth. Conversely this means that the opportunity to obtain gainful employment must be conceded to every member of society. (Beck, Bonss and Lau 2003: 4)

The other facet of first modernity is what they call the 'functional differentiation' of society and of lifecourses within it. Increased specialization and complexity of social functions were seen to achieve 'a better calibration of ends with means'. After the turbulence of early industrialization, a stable social environment was established that sought to reconcile or naturalize the existing class divisions and family formations within the unified boundaries of the nation-state. The culmination of first modernity was exemplified by writers such as Marshall and Titmuss, who believed that modern society leads inevitably to the realization of universal social rights and social security while maintaining equality of opportunity within a market economy.[3]

The final feature of 'Modernity 1' they refer to as 'a programmatic individualization' in which, though people are theoretically free and equal, 'their freedom and equality are moulded by social institutions – for example the sexual division of labour – that are in many respects coercive' (Beck, Bonss and Lau 2003: 4). Despite rhetoric to the contrary, ascription still determined one's fate. The social class that people were born into remained a clear and pervasive boundary determining access not only to the material surplus of the economy but also to the cultural practices that supported and strengthened those boundaries operating progressively across public, communal and domestic domains.

Modernity 2 is a response to the challenges and dynamics of Modernity 1. The intensification of individualization through the successes of the welfare state (improved education, housing, health care and social security) has eroded many of the ascriptive patterns of collective life. A breakdown in the full employment society leads to a decline in the significance of continuous, gainful employment, as 'status, consumption and social security choices have – to some extent – become progressively independent of income, and thus of labour force participation' (Beck, Bonss and Lau 2003: 6–7). For Beck and his colleagues this 'revolution through side effects' has created a new set of problems confronting society, which 'call into question the traditional rule by experts in economics, politics and science' while '[t]he questions have come to appear stronger than any answers' (Beck 2000: 21–2).

Modernity 2 is characterized by reflexivity, which, for Beck, is modernity's response to the unintended consequences of its own actions. The successful resolution of the conflicts that modernity has itself constructed (predominantly the conflicts of class and gender) has the effect of dissolving the very boundaries that provided the framework of modern, corporate society. The dominance of the state, the work place and the nuclear family are equally challenged. The internal structure of classes and class society lose their explicit salience in organizing social identities, leading paradoxically to widening social inequalities as the mechanisms for ordering and organizing income have lost much of their normative capacity. In Modernity 1, the stability of individual subjectivity was presaged upon the institutionalized boundaries of the modern life cycle. In Modernity 2 'the individual can no longer be conceived as a stable and unchangeable subject, but rather [appears] as a "quasi subject", the result *as well as* the producer of its networks, situation, location and form' (Beck, Bonss and Lau 2003: 25).

The greater fluidity of the individual lifecourse that characterizes Modernity 2 arises from processes that were already set in train within Modernity 1: namely, the need of corporate capitalist enterprises to expand both production and consumption. By the first decades of the twentieth century, consumerism emerged as 'an aggressive device of corporate survival' (Ewen 1976: 54). It was promoted as the most practicable route to achieving a democracy, but a democracy based upon mass consumption and one that legitimated the dominance of the market. Though articulation of this corporate philosophy appeared early in the century, it was not until after the establishment of the post-Second World War welfare state had guaranteed security from impoverishment for all that a society of mass consumption could be fully supported and sustained. In the process of achieving a society of mass consumption, the demands of consumers had to be maintained by rising incomes and widening choices. To ensure increasing consumer choice, it is necessary to increase the opportunities for individual households and for individuals within households to differentiate themselves from each other – to foster 'an adherence to the pluralism of commodities' (Ewen 1976: 90). Within this 'consumers' republic', the solidarities of class are replaced by what Cohen has called 'citizen consumers' (L. Cohen 2003: 18–60).

The processes that constitute mass consumer society saw their first full expression in the USA in the inter-war years as corporate organizations struggled to overcome the earlier collective forms of popular culture that had flourished in the USA toward the end of the nineteenth and early twentieth century. Already visible in the immediate post-war era, this new culture was epitomized in the development of suburban communities built around the sites of mass consumption that constituted 'the Mall'. As Cohen has observed, 'Whereas once work and family had dictated residence, now increasingly consumption – of homes, goods, services and leisure – did' (L. Cohen 2003: 197).

The focus upon the family household as a site of consumption for whose personal benefit an ever greater array of black and white goods were displayed as the visible markers of status was quickly recognized by US social commentators (Marcuse 1964; Packard 1957). Despite the critical stance taken by those who believed that American society was being seduced into a state of consumer stupefication, the appeal of the new consumer society continued to grow, and it soon extended across the Atlantic. In Europe fears were expressed that a vulgar materialism created by this new American consumer lifestyle would swamp 'European culture'. While such fears were widely expounded in Britain, France and Italy, the politicians in these countries were equally eager to let their people know that they, too, 'had never had it so good'.

Despite the growing affluence and conformity of post-war societies, they could not achieve social closure. Class-based conflicts continued, while new generational conflicts arose as the post-war 'baby boom' generation emerged as an affluent and well-educated segment whose allegiance to their class was diminished in direct relation to their dislike of its complacency. Consumer society, which previously had been confined by the boundaries of class and gender, now treated those boundaries as increasingly cultural and therefore permeable. New social movements fostered a different political agenda, calling for a broader recognition of women's rights and those of other 'repressed minorities' that Modernity 1 had been unable, or unwilling, to assimilate into its class-based framework. A growing equality of opportunity in education diminished occupational barriers, most noticeably for women, leading to increased rates of participation of women within the economy. Changes in the nature of work have led to an increase in both intermediate and middle-class occupations, to the point where the majority of the population in developed societies neither are nor describe themselves as 'working-class' (Kingston 2000: 87–100; K. Roberts 2001: 70). As the personal became the focus for a new style of politics, it ceased to matter so much what job one did. Instead, it began to matter far more what other identities one had and how much they had to be hidden, masked or denied in order to fit into the 'system': whether one was gay, disabled or a member of a religious or subcultural ethnic grouping.

The shifting nature of contemporary occupational categories, the fragmentation of working lives, the disconnectedness between the working experiences of past and present generations, and the increased permeability and physical dislocatedness of work, home and the public sphere are central features of the new modernity. This 'necessary' fragmentation now extends beyond working life, influencing present and future cohorts of young and old, those not yet in the labour market and those retiring from it. More and more, 'objective' forms of social categorization like age or gender are dismissed as little more than arbitrary social constructions, created by some corporate cultural megalith so that age-denying or gender-bending products can be sold, implicitly upsetting the balance of respect and value associated with one binary opposition over another. 'Classism' joins racism, sexism, ageism and disablism as merely one of the many divides that separate those who may and those who may not be recognized and given respect. Not only is the authority of class and gender subverted, so too is the very nature of 'nature' itself.

Modernity 2 and the Post-Modernized Lifecourse

Hakim has argued that 'affluent and liberal modern societies provide opportunities for diverse lifestyle preferences to be fully realized' (Hakim 2000: 273). For her, this is most noticeably evident in the work–lifestyle preferences of women, who as a result of equal opportunities and the contraceptive revolution, confront 'genuine choices' as to what to do with their lives – whether to work, be home-centred, or mix and modify the two. The general inference from her argument is that the existence of preferences extends beyond the issue of women and paid employment. She argues more generally for the growing importance of attitudes, values and preferences in shaping the modern life cycle, which she sees as one of the main tenets of 'preference theory'. As Hakim herself notes, these views accord closely with those of Beck, Giddens and theories of 'reflexive modernization'. The underlying premiss of preference theory is individual agency – social actors choosing to act. The individual life project, central to the discourse of Modernity 2, requires the exercise of choice as a constant flow of action over the lifecourse.

Hakim is aware that these changes, which are taking place within the context of successive generations of men and women, extend across all sectors of society and cover a wider domain of activities than simply the choice between staying at home or going to work. Exposure to the opportunities of preference has increased substantially since the 'cultural revolution' of the Sixties, as an economy of desires began to displace an economy of needs (Hakim 2000: 43–83). Lifestyle choices within rich modern societies, she argues, relate less closely to income and occupational class, tending instead to reflect generational shifts in attitudes and values that have been realized within liberal welfare capitalist societies during the post-war era. These choices result in a progressively less stable lifecourse. It becomes harder to predict the consequences arising from the increasing exercise of choice across lengthening periods of life. This can extend from whether or not to go to college to whether to work full time, part time or not at all. It can include whether to marry at a younger or later age, or not to marry at all; whether to have one, several or no children, and whether to stay with one partner, change partners or live alone, etc. The choices are ever proliferating.

The institutionalization of the lifecourse within Modernity 1 was achieved by the progressive involvement of the state in the redistribution of resources across the lifespan as much as across social classes. Government social expenditure, particularly on education and social protection, rose steadily throughout the twentieth century, most notably in the post-war period, from the 1950s to the 1970s (Mullard 1993). The result was a more predictable, institutionalized childhood, greater consistency in the period when children grow up and leave home, a narrowing of the child-bearing years, and a clearer common demarcation between when working life begins and when it ends. This 'homogenisation of experiences . . . ran across class boundaries as well as within them' (M. Anderson 1985: 86). Institutionalizing the modern lifecourse was a precursor to its individualization. As Beck has pointed out, the growing influence of the state in ensuring a more predictable lifecourse had the unintended consequence of replacing 'status-influenced, class, cultural or familial biographical rhythms . . . by institutional biographical patterns' (Beck 1990: 133–4). The decline of the mediating influences of class, community and family rendered these newly individualized lives ever more dependent upon the market, a market that was itself undergoing a profound transformation toward a system of lean production. By providing predictability, the state made possible the exercise of choice. Those choices are exercised now in conditions of greater uncertainty and more distant outcomes.

Recently, there has been a shift in studies of inequality toward what has been called a 'lifecourse perspective' (Leisering and Liebfried 1999; Mayer and Schoplin 1989; Sorensen 2000). This perspective recognizes that variability in the material and social outcomes of individual lives can no longer be construed as stable, fixed social positions. Considerable empirical research on the longitudinal instability of household incomes suggests that a focus upon occupational mobility (or lack of it) no longer directly translates into variations in the material well-being outcomes of either individuals or households (Burkhauser and Poupore 1997; DiPrete and MacManus 2000). While it is still the case that corporatist and social democratic welfare states exercise an influence in reducing the variability of outcomes across the lifecourse, the extent of that influence is being modified in the face of mounting pressures from global financial institutions and transnational corporations. As DiPrete and his colleagues have noted, 'there has been considerable speculation in recent years that Europe will be forced by global competition to make its labor markets more "flexible" and hence more individualistic in order to save its economy from stagnation' (DiPrete et al. 1997: 352). The turn toward a more liberal welfare state such as that exemplified by the UK, Ireland, the USA and New Zealand can only serve to further reduce the potential for de-commodification, tying individual work and post-working life ever more closely together. The clearly institutionalized divisions of education, work, marriage and retirement are becoming more permeable, as patterns of income and expenditure are negotiated throughout the secured uncertainties of the post-modern lifecourse.

The New Structuration of Ageing

In Modernity 2, class as a social identity no longer serves to underpin the mobilizing power of social institutions to gain greater access to, and influence over, society's surplus. The historical alignment between workers' rights and the right to retire with a pension allowed old age to be treated as a site that could best be defined by, and articulated through, class conflict. By exercising class power over the allocation of resources for old age, the working-classes' political institutions established their claim upon old age as a 'social good' paid for by the wages foregone by workers earlier in their working lives. Framed in this way as deferred wages, the pension income of most working people remained at a relatively low rate throughout the first half of the twentieth century. Since the 1960s incremental improvements in pension payments have sustained a link between wages earned earlier in life and pension incomes later in life, which has meant that pension income in most developed countries has continued to rise, as have the material assets of pensioners. As Robert Brenner recently has pointed out, the rise in property values has outstripped the rise in equities, helping to sustain record levels of borrowing (Brenner 2004). Rising levels of home ownership and increased 'notional' pension wealth seem to have transformed the hypothesized post-war 'affluent workers' into newly 'embourgeoisied' pensioners. If the intention of welfare reformers and trades unions was to 'de-commodify' old age by securing a universal social wage that would let working men (and their wives) retire from paid employment with a degree of material ease in their later years, then many of these intentions have been fulfilled. At the same time, the nature of working life and its connections to later life have undergone significant changes. The de-commodification of later life has turned out not to be quite what it seemed.

The first change of note is that, in a significant number of countries, state pension income has been supplemented by the additional contributions made by workers and their employers to an occupational pension. In Britain, this has altered the character of the flat-rate state pension by turning it into a poverty-preventing payment which maintains the aged as a marginal class whose social position is not dissimilar to that of the aged deserving poor. Conversely, the retirement income of those workers with histories of continued full-time employment and steadily rising wages has improved considerably, making their retirement much more equivalent to that of the average 'working man'. Such dual pensioners are in some ways more completely 'de-commodified' than most, since they receive a similar wage without occupying the exploited position of wage labour. The retirement income of those still in part-time employment after retirement age, and of those who have invested in private pension plans or made other investments, place many of them in equally favoured positions. These positions exist in sharp contrast to that of the retired widow living on social security payments in rented accommodation.

In short, the class position of retired people has diversified, creating a wider variety of positions than was ever intended by the welfare state reformers. Some pensioners appear to operate as *rentier* capitalists living off the proceeds of returns upon investments; others function like members of a marginalized welfare class, modern-day paupers whose exposure to the market is mediated by their perceived needs. Others occupy a free-floating 'déclassé' position, receiving a partially de-commodified retirement income that, though treated as deferred wages, is connected purely symbolically to the labour that created this notional surplus.

The second change is in the social reality that is fragmenting the potential of pensioners to articulate and act upon a coherent class identity. This is common to many groups of people in a period of reflexive modernization. For most people, Lenin's question 'Who whom?' no longer permits any ready answer. Working lives have become more flexible, and relations between employers and employees more individualized. Lifelong learning has overtaken learning to labour, while the importance of collective arrangements over working *practices* has declined. In an economy dominated by shareholder value and supra-national governance, the existence of necessary interconnections between profit, productivity, pay and pensions can no longer be assumed. By this we mean that there are now many avenues by which the soundness and stability of pay and pension arrangements can be undermined, whether through miscalculated employers' 'pension holidays', deliberately or accidentally mismanaged pension funds, or the instability of financial markets. Just as the productivity of an enterprise no longer guarantees that 'global conditions' will not make the enterprise unprofitable, risk management of investment funds may be grossly miscalculated, while even national agreements over the terms and conditions of PAYGO contributory pension schemes may be radically changed by the demands of supranational agreements such as the Euro stability pact. While we are not arguing that the capitalist system has been replaced by a 'post-capitalist' economy, the way that capitalism operates in Modernity 2 is sufficiently removed from the earlier model of industrial capitalism that set in train these changes that it requires some additional term to qualify its new form. Whether this is a disorganized, turbo or post-modern form of capitalism, it throws up novel phenomena that cannot simply be read off from antecedent formations and structures.

The third change is the growing salience of consumption as the basis for a 'mass' culture that unites workers and managers, those at work and those who either have not yet joined the work-force or have left it. Most Western economies successfully increased their Gross National Product in the decades after the Second World War. The profits that were created during this period were made primarily through manufacturing productivity, effective marketing, and better sales and delivery, along with improved terms and conditions for labour. The result was a growing surplus to which workers were able to gain access. Access to that surplus altered household consumption, ensuring that the majority of the population of the Western world had more and cheaper food, better housing and household amenities, a greater supply of fuel and energy, and a wider range of leisure goods than ever before. As a consequence, consumption over and above the necessities for sustaining life and home has come to dominate production at a cultural, if not at a purely material, level.

Participation in post-war mass culture is not evenly shared across gender, age or class divisions. Neither is it restricted to particular birth cohorts, particular income groups or particular classes. Modernity 2 is the Modernity of the 'consumer republic', developed along cultural vectors whose trajectories are not easily mapped and whose origins and consequences are ever more heterogeneous. While age, gender, occupation, income and wealth continue to provide sources of social distinction, it is no longer clear whether those distinctions define or disguise people's identities. Inserted into the lives of all but the most marginal are practices and discourses of identity and differentiation whose origins can no longer be mapped on to their explicit or implicit position within the labour market. This disconnectedness renders more problematic the position of those who cease to occupy a formal position within the labour market. In the next chapter we shall explore what this means for class as a contextual structure shaping ageing, retirement and later life.

3

The Nature of Class in Later Life

The history of older people's poverty in industrialized societies has allowed social class to translate directly from working life into retirement. This is less easy to assert now in the light of rising affluence among large sections of the retired population that we described in chapter 1. Such relative affluence has been made possible by the shift from social assistance to replacement income, from structuring old age support as social protection against immiseration to ensuring that significant numbers of older people have access to resources in their own right. In Britain, the motor for many of these changes has been the growth in occupational and private pensions, which have gradually shifted the position of the retired from that of a residual welfare class to being an integral part of the class structure itself. The steady expansion of white-collar work and the service sector and the decline of traditional manual occupations altered the class composition of the UK during the course of the second half of the twentieth century. These and other changes have increased the diversity of resources available to people upon retirement, rendering later life almost as fragmented as working life itself. This fragmentation of material resources and social identities leads, on the one hand, to a growing inequality in later life, and on the other, to a continuing engagement with consumer society.

Industrialization and the Impoverishment of Age

From the sixteenth century onwards, European Poor Laws sought to formalize the responsibility of the local community to support those of its inhabitants who had fallen on hard times. Becoming a widow or an orphan, as well as illness and infirmity, were recognized as potential causes of indigence. Within this framework of formal support, 'agedness' became a predominant category of need. As agrarian capitalism was superseded by industrialization as the dominant mode of production, the new factory system and the mechanization of manual labour caused difficulties for older workers as they demanded either a rapid pace of work or intense, sustained physical labour. The emphasis on the productivity rather than the skills of labour meant that the ageing of the worker became a potentially important factor in undermining the efficiency of industry. The associated process of urbanization removed alternative opportunities for self-sufficiency that had previously existed in rural areas, based upon ownership of, or access to, land and property.[1]

The rise in late-life unemployment coupled with the trend toward workers seeking a 'family wage' placed strains upon the parish or commune model of Poor Law support. These traditional systems of support for old age had developed against a background of the old regime's 'one class' society, based upon the links between the land, the local gentry and the local clergy. As the Poor Law system was confronted by the new problems of industrial poverty, it elicited growing criticisms from conservatives and reformers alike. Despite the austerity with which it was applied, the Poor Law system represented rising 'cost' to the state, a cost that yielded few benefits. It rapidly became apparent that the system was failing to address the needs of those excluded by an industrial mode of production.

By the end of the nineteenth century, the problem of poverty had been reformulated: 'Reformers at the end of the century were prone to see poverty not as a single monolith, but as an array of particular problems related to the life cycle of individuals and to the ups and downs of the economy' (Brundage 2002: 131–2). This life cycle model of poverty highlighted the vulnerable position of older people within the new economy. There was extensive discussion of the need for an old age pension to ensure that those no longer able to find work could live out the remaining part of their lives without the stigma of pauperism. Old age poverty was fast becoming endemic. In any one year, in England, between a third and a quarter

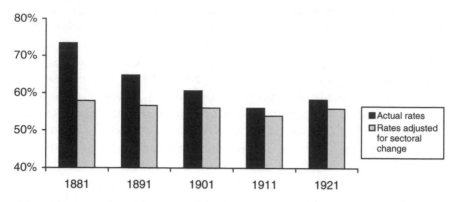

Figure 3.1   Labour force participation rates of older men (England and Wales, 1881–1921). Source: Johnson 1994.

of the population aged 65 and over found themselves recipients of outdoor or indoor poor relief (Nield 1898) as labour force participation rates amongst older men continued steadily to decline. This decline was due to the rise of industrialization and the demise of agriculture as a labour-intensive sector of the economy. If these changes in the sectoral composition of the UK work-force had not occurred, as Johnson has shown, there would have been virtually *no* decline in older men's work-force participation rates throughout the period between 1880 and 1920 (see fig. 3.1).

Following several years of debate, the British government finally passed legislation creating old age pensions in 1908. Based upon general taxation, the pension 'was not intended to provide an income adequate to survival but to supplement and to encourage saving and the support available from relatives and others' (Thane 2000: 223). It was not to be given to those who had previously been idle or who had received poor relief earlier in their working life; nor was it made available to those with a record of drunkenness or who possessed the status of aliens or wives of aliens. Its impact upon the economic position of the older population was quite small. There was no mass exit from the labour force, and significant numbers of older people still relied upon outdoor relief (in the form of public assistance). Its cultural significance was more important, however, for it reformalized the state's categorization of old age from pauper to pensioner.

In continental Europe, similar effects were achieved, albeit through different mechanisms. Almost three decades before the old age pension was introduced in Britain, Bismarck had established a state old age pension in Imperial Germany. This was part of a broader national system introducing contributory social insurance to cover unemployment due to sickness, disability and old age. The old age pension was low, and older workers leaving the work-force, chose, wherever possible, to receive the higher rate disability benefits. In the twenty years following the introduction of the old age pension, the number of old age pensioners in Germany actually fell, while the numbers of older people claiming outdoor relief continued to rise (Ritter 1986: 191). In France, though Napoleon III established a non-contributory old age pension scheme in 1851, it was confined to France's civil servants. A nation-wide provision for old age was not attempted until much later, when, in 1905, legislation was passed guaranteeing old age assistance payments to the aged who were unable to work. A non-compulsory contributory old age pension scheme was established five years later. But in neither case was there universal coverage; nor was the funding set at a level to encourage older people to leave the labour market (Diebolt and Reimat 1997). These continental European old age pension systems, based upon mutual contributions by employers and employees, paid out pensions that fell well below wages, primarily because it took some time for the funds to build up as successive cohorts of workers started paying into the schemes. Although these early state pension schemes took some of the punitive and arbitrary nature out of Poor Law payments, they offered in return few material benefits and were generally insufficient to fend off poverty, particularly in times of economic hardship. Wage labour continued to form the economic mainstay for the majority of older families. The legislation that spread across Europe in the decades before and after the First World War created the symbolic character of the old age pensioner, but did little in practice to transform their situation. In the period just prior to 1914, old age pensions in Britain and Germany represented less than 20 per cent of average working people's wages. 'The aged' remained the residual category to which they had been assigned by the earlier Poor Law system (Orloff 1993: 136).

Meantime, the position of the working class was consolidated. With the establishment of universal male suffrage, the working class became more visible as a political force, whose representatives argued for increased wages to maintain their independence and avoid incorporation into the state. Although marked inequalities in earnings persisted between the classes, wages increased across the board, and standards of living improved (Routh 1965; Scholliers 1989). Across Europe membership of mutual societies grew, as working men sought to insure their own and their families' future outside the framework of either the state or their employer (Dreyfus 1996). In Britain, workers began to benefit from the growth of newly introduced occupational pension schemes. By the 1930s, there were over two and a half million employees in employer-based pension schemes in both the public and private sectors (Hannah 1985: 350). In continental Europe similar private occupational pension schemes emerged, modelled upon those elaborated in the Anglo-Saxon world (Wiedenbeck and den Osgood 1996: 71). However, with the exception of Holland and Switzerland, the level of coverage was much less extensive, due to the establishment of various state-mediated earnings-related social insurance schemes. The economic crisis of the 1930s threw many of these assumptions of collective 'self-reliance' into confusion. Global recession and mass unemployment dealt a fatal blow to such ideals as a new mood of corporatism emerged across Europe. While the contradictory forms that this took in different countries – National Socialism and fascism in Germany and Italy, popular frontism in France, and national government in Britain – they all shared in a common retreat into the nation. While this retreat contributed to the onset of the Second World War, it also created the conditions for the eventual emergence of the post-war welfare state. Within this newly fashioned, national social compact, retirement would become institutionalized as the universal condition of later life.

American Exceptionalism?

Things proceeded somewhat differently on the other side of the Atlantic. At the end of the nineteenth century, the majority of men aged 65 and older in the USA were still working, most being employed as farmers (Costa 1998: 86). The problems of an industrialized labour force were concentrated in the north-eastern states. On farms, 80 per cent of older men continued to work, while almost half of the urban working class had stopped work by the age of 65 (Costa 1998: 23). There was no system of national assistance. State Poor Law arrangements provided some relief for the indigent aged who were without alternative means of support, but provision was much more limited than was the case in Western Europe (Orloff 1993: 141–3). The number of veterans of the Civil War who began to receive military pensions in the 1870s increased significantly after the Dependent Pension Act of 1890 was passed. This law entitled any veteran of the Union armed forces to claim a pension if they became unfit for manual labour. The Veterans' Pension came to function as a kind of federal old age pension, and by 1910 about a quarter of the US over-65 population was reliant upon it to provide an income for their old age.[2]

Despite the absence of any federal legislation on pensions in the USA, work-force participation rates of older men declined. By 1920, 40 per cent of men aged 65 and over were no longer working, a figure that was not much lower than in Europe. Because of higher real wages and greater opportunities for self-employment, the existence of a relatively well-off rural population, the early development of private union- and employer-funded pension schemes, and the support that was provided by the Veterans' Pension, the economic circumstances of US retirees were generally better than was the case in Europe. Surveys conducted in the mid-1920s suggest that nearly half of the urban US population over 65 had assets and potential earnings equal to or greater than average workers' wages (Gratton 1996: 54). Neither before nor after the First World War was there the level of agitation for a national system of social insurance as there was in Europe. Opposition to all forms of federal state provisions continued to be voiced by local politicians, labour organizations and employers alike. According to Theda Skocpol, interest in European style social insurance policies was confined to a small number of 'social scientists or labor analysts . . . occup[ying] a variety of university, government and corporate positions' (Skocpol 1995:

141). Although several states proposed legislation introducing old age pensions before 1929, very few ever reached the statute book.

The Wall Street Crash and the economic depression that followed provided the spur for change. Unemployment had always been a problem, despite the prosperity of the 1920s. It rose dramatically from half a million in 1928 to over 8 million in 1931, reaching a peak in 1933 of around 15 million men – one-third of the male work-force (Piven and Cloward 1993: 48–61). The impact of the Depression was much greater and was much more focused in particular industries and cities. Manufacturing industry was especially badly affected. Since older workers were disproportionately concentrated in farming, the non-household service sector, crafts and the professions, the Depression tended to affect younger workers more adversely than older ones. Writing in *Vanity Fair* in 1931, Bruce Barton half-jokingly suggested as a potential solution to the economic crisis that 'every man and woman in the United States be retired from work at the age of 45 on a pension amounting to one half of his or her average earnings in the preceding five years . . . creat[ing] a special automatic class of consumers' (cited in Mitchell 2000: 85). Such ideas found a more serious articulation in the Townsendite movement. A retired physician, Dr Francis Townsend, began a popular campaign to provide a tax-funded old age pension of $150 per month from the federal government to all US citizens aged 60 and over, which he proposed funding from a 2 per cent tax on all market transactions (Mitchell 2000). These proposals influenced Roosevelt and his advisors when they were formulating their New Deal legislation, including the introduction of a new old age Social Security programme that ensured payments of around $30 dollars a month, after retirement, based upon employer and employee contributions. The legislation was aimed at enabling older workers to retire, creating opportunities for work for younger men with families. The New Deal was not primarily directed at preventing the pauperization of older people. It reflected the government's very real need to address the social unrest that the Depression precipitated. As Piven and Cloward have pointed out, 'Many began to define their hardships, not as an individual fate, but as a collective disaster, not as a mark of individual failure, but as a fault of the "system"' (Piven and Cloward 1993: 61). Private charity and local state and municipal authorities were clearly unable to cope. As mass disorder spread across America, the old economic order became polarized.

The new Social Security legislation sought to buy off the growing militancy of the workers and the unemployed. Roosevelt did not want Social Security to be considered as welfare. What he sought to establish was a federally run pension system that resembled a private pension plan. People would pay in to a defined benefits scheme, earning an annuity that reflected the history of their contributions. Old age assistance continued as a means-tested benefit to the indigent aged. This was referred to as a pension. By framing Social Security as an annuitized, funded scheme, the 1935 Act preserved a distinction that had been already articulated by the private insurance industry, between a pensioner, 'one who is dependent upon the bounty of another', and an annuitant, 'one who receives or is entitled to receive an annuity' (Klein 2003: 76). The US system of Social Security set itself a different goal from that associated with the social insurance schemes of pre-war Europe: not the amelioration of indigence but rather the maintenance in later life of 'the distributional profile of incomes and benefits generated by the . . . market' (Skocpol 1995: 137). Though Roosevelt wanted to avoid creating an 'unfunded gratuitous poverty scheme' such as that proposed by Townsend and his followers, the spirit behind the slogan of the Townsendite movement – '*Youth for Work/Age for Leisure*' – remained in the reflationary intentions of the legislation (Graebner 1980: 197). The New Deal cemented the relationship between work and old age, ensuring that the latter was funded through the deferred wages of working life. Only those who had been marginal to the formal economy when younger retained a marginal status in old age as 'welfare pension recipients'. Supported by the middle and working classes alike, 'Social Security' has remained one of the most popular federal policies in the USA, and a key source for the elderly population's relative affluence after the war.

Beveridge and Beyond

The Second World War was a total war, involving whole populations of the most industrialized nations in the world. The need to build a consensus within the nation was a priority both for military victory and for reconstruction after the war. In Britain, this took the form of William Beveridge's plans for a comprehensive system of National Insurance that would protect the population from the worst excesses of the free market that had been all too evident in pre-war Europe. The Marshall Plan for European reconstruction fostered the development of the modern welfare state throughout the devastated Western world. In practice this meant that social insurance policies were enacted across Western Europe.

How did this policy affect the connections between working life and old age? Did the modern welfare state create a de-commodified, free-floating class of pensioners, distanced from the divisions and inequalities of working life? Or did it succeed in more comprehensively institutionalizing old age as a marginal category of welfare dependency? Part of the answer to these questions can be found through an examination of the post-war British experience. At the time when the post-war Labour government introduced universal pay-as-you-go old age pensions, one in three workers were already contributing to an occupational pension scheme (Hannah 1986). Flat-rate universal pensions were intended to establish solidarity between classes and generations. At the same time, the architects of the Beveridgian welfare state were never in doubt that the universal pension was intended principally to alleviate poverty and not to create a new leisure class in retirement. As Beveridge himself put it, 'it is dangerous to be in any way lavish to old age' (Macnicol and Blaikie 1989: 36). Although differing in their interpretation of subsistence, the Trades Union Congress also supported the government's focus upon improving the opportunities for younger people to find work and the conditions of those in work. Their concern was initially with competition in the labour market. Subsequently the unions were more concerned to negotiate for higher wages and greater employer contributions to industry-wide occupational pension schemes and seemed reasonably content with a flat-rate system that was singularly unsuccessful in reducing pensioner poverty (Thane 2000: 380–1).

For a crucial period in the twentieth century, trades unions played a significant role in articulating the interests of the working class to secure an adequate income throughout life. This role was articulated in two separate if related ways: through their role as intermediaries in negotiating the sectional interests of particular groups of workers, and as part of the collective debate about welfare and the elimination of want and poverty. This brings us to a central paradox, most apparent in the British case but with echoes in the experience of continental Europe. In an orthodox social democratic approach, as advocated by trades unions, the articulation of the interests of class should see its embodiment in a universalistic welfare state based upon egalitarianism. The interests of the working class should be represented as the interests of the whole society, and there should be as little inequality as possible. In particular, there should be no unfair consequences of location inside or outside the labour market. While this was conceived mainly with the idea of protecting the male wage-earner and maintaining the domestic division of labour in the family, in time (and particularly in the Nordic countries) this was extended to women and to members of discriminated against groups. The paradox is that the post-war welfare state did not create equality in late-life incomes, nor did it do much to lessen the impact of labour market position upon the distribution of retirement incomes.

This is in large part the consequence of the contradictory positions held by the institutional representatives of the working class, as both local intermediaries and as the political voice of a putative 'universal' class. The history of the twentieth century saw trade union politics move from a total rejection of the economic system of capitalism to an accommodation with it. Throughout the post-war social compact, this accommodation was represented, first, through the achievement of universal social rights (pensions, health care and sickness and unemployment benefits) and subsequently through growing productivity and affluence. While the nature of this accommodation has taken different forms in different countries, it shared the common belief that capitalism was capable of being reformed out of existence. It was widely believed that social reform could mitigate the adverse effects of labour being a commodity that was bought and sold. Instead of abolishing class society, the consequences of class membership were to be progressively attenuated.

In his *The Three Worlds of Welfare Capitalism* Esping-Andersen analysed the reforms of the post-war welfare state, categorizing the welfare regime of each state on the basis of its capacity to introduce rights and support 'de-commodification'. By de-commodification, Esping-Andersen means the ability of a person to maintain a livelihood without recourse to the market. As he writes, 'a minimal definition must entail that citizens can freely, and without potential loss of job, income or general welfare, opt out of work when they themselves consider it necessary' (Esping-Andersen 1990: 23). Obviously, most welfare states do not score highly on this criterion. The divisions between social assistance, social insurance and what Esping-Andersen calls 'Beveridgian' welfare states create the foundations for different forms of strati-fication. This is particularly important in relation to retirement pensions. The social assistance model is designed to stigmatize recipients through principles such as means testing, making access to the status of 'pensioner' contingent upon its marginality. In con-trast, the social insurance model consolidates divisions between wage-earners by preserving in later life much of the differentials that corresponded with their earlier market position. Although the Beveridgian model promises maximum de-commodification through its premiss of universalism; as Esping-Andersen notes, 'the solidarity of flat-rate universalism presumes a historically peculiar class structure, one in which the vast majority of the population are the "little people" for whom a modest, albeit egalitarian, benefit may be considered adequate' (Esping-Andersen 1990: 25). It is not surprising that growing numbers of the middle class and the more affluent members of the working class turned to private schemes to escape this fate and effectively created a dual system of retirement income.

The post-war welfare state represented an attempt to shift the position of retired people from that of a vulnerable welfare class, dependent upon 'assistance' to that of a free floating class, capable of participating in society without relying upon the productive system.[3] It only ever partly succeeded. Before and after the estab-lishment of the welfare state, trades unions continued to pursue their sectional interests in securing a more comfortable retirement for their constituent members. In Australia, Britain and the United States this took place outside the remit of the state through collective bargaining over occupational pension rights. In continental Europe, the focus moved to preserving the position of working people after retirement. In Germany this was done through indexing pensions to wages and 'ensuring that the employed person's individual situation during his working life continues correspondingly when he receives a pension' (Kurt Jantz, cited in Zöllner 1982: 66), while in France it was achieved by creating 'a mosaic of special autonomous or supplementary schemes alongside a general scheme' (Saint-Jours 1982: 131). This model has in many ways proved a successful strategy, resulting in the gradual extension of either funded or 'pay-as-you-go' (PAYGO) occupational pensions and, as wages have risen, higher employer contributions and a generally higher level of replacement income in later life. Middle-class staff associations, who were used to defending an occupational stratum have seen their own aspirations extended to larger sections of previously working-class employees. They now find themselves presenting a common, if at times differentiated, front in the pursuit of improved terms in both private and public sectors.

The early post-war welfare states ensured against pauperism but still left the majority of pensioners close to the margins of poverty. As employment prospects in later life shrank, and as the combination of state and occupational pensions rose in value, retirement became not just a universal opportunity but a near universal experience. By 1977, 90 per cent of those over 65 were 'retired'. In Britain, poverty levels among pensioners had dropped to below 25 per cent (Goodman, Mick and Shephard 2003: fig. 5.2). The majority of newly retired men (58 per cent) were in receipt of both a state and an occupational (private) pension. In Germany, relative poverty rates among those aged 65 and over fell even further, to just over 10 per cent. A similar fall in poverty rates amongst the retired population was evident in France. Despite its compromises, the 'modern' welfare state system was beginning to deliver a longer, healthier and richer later life than had been the experience of many pensioners during their earlier working lives. Significant numbers of retired people were successfully transformed into members of a de-commodified, free-floating class removed from the exigencies of their earlier working lives while still sharing in the growing affluence of the 'golden years' of welfare capitalism.

Globalization and the Individualization of Later Life

From the 1980s onwards, the welfare state came under pressure from both within and without. A common source of tension was the growing internationalization of markets and their impact on national economies.[4] In the wake of the oil crises of the 1970s and the collapse of the Bretton Woods agreement, transnational flows of capital increased greatly. Greater capital mobility reduced the capacity of nation-states to control the movement of capital in and out of their respective countries, leaving them exposed to the effects of international competition. In response, governments everywhere sought to control public expenditure to maintain their national competitiveness, manifested as an ability to retain and attract both domestic and international capital.[5] A common response was to turn toward 'the market' as the means of reducing the pressures on public expenditure arising from the growth of unemployment and the increase in the size of the retired population. Although the extent of this 'turn to the market' has varied from country to country, it has been consistent in its direction. One consequence is a growing individualization of the means of sustaining income protection in later life as the situation in postwork comes to mirror working life. At the same time developments in state welfare provision concentrate more and more on poverty prevention (Scharpf 2000: 222).

The relative equalization of later life experience and its economic underpinning that was achieved between the 1950s and the 1970s began to unravel during the 1980s (Johnson and Stears 1995). But the result was not that the majority of the retired grew poorer in consequence. In fact, the gap between the average working wage and average retirement income narrowed during the last two decades of the twentieth century, as rising pensioner incomes outpaced the more modest increases in wage incomes. Growing material inequalities in later life were accompanied by increasing opportunities for people in later life to pursue retirement lifestyles beyond the earlier institutionalized boundaries of 'old age' (Disney and Whitehouse 2001: 60). Patterns of income, wealth and expenditure marked out new categories of retired people, whose lifestyles were no longer defined by the social stratification created by welfare policy. The idea that later life should be represented by the 'old age pensioner' no longer matched the reality. By the 1990s, income for the poorest 20 per cent of UK pensioners was almost entirely made up from public transfers (old age pensions and supplementary benefits). In contrast, two thirds of the income of the richest 20 per cent was derived from private sources in the form of occupational pensions, personal pensions, annuities and other sources of investment income, as well as on the returns on property (Johnson and Stears 1995; Department of Work and Pensions 2003).

This new reality not only chimed with neo-liberal thinking on the consequences of demographic ageing in the UK, but also reflected the global concerns of international finance. In 1994 the World Bank internationalized the problem, outlining the case for an impending 'old age crisis' requiring urgent political action and structural reform in all countries. It proposed its now familiar 'three-pillar approach' of state, occupational and private pensions as the best way of spreading the financial risk of securing an adequate income in later life. The bank argued that individuals needed to take greater responsibility for insuring the effective redistribution of their earnings across their own lifecourse. In essence, the World Bank asked governments to reject the idea, dominant for much of the post-war period, that collective state-funded provision should meet the demand for income main-tenance in later life that was now the expectation of growing numbers of older people (World Bank 1994).

It is paradoxical that part of the reason for the 'crisis' in pen-sions was the very success of de-commodification. As prosperity has become part of everyday experience for large sections of the population, a growing amount of revenue has to be redistributed to ensure parity between workers and non-workers. The policy agenda is no longer about relieving poverty and want, but about ensuring social inclusion in a consumerist society. Growing reluc-tance in the UK for the state to subsidize consumption has led to the articulation of a new 'social' compact between citizens and the state (Bauman 1998). In this newly sought accommodation, citizens are expected to act as the agent of their own ageing, deter-mining their income in later life through savings and investments made during the course of working life and beyond. A growing number of countries have introduced pension reforms, which are either aimed at constraining state-mediated entitlements or are intended to induce or even require their citizens to participate in the World Bank's 'second' and 'third pillar' pension arrangements. While continental European nations have not completely abandoned their social insurance pension systems, the 'corporatist' approach is seen as a serious threat to the viability of their own and the global economy. High incomes in retirement, according to the World Bank, should emerge from an active engagement with national and international capital. They should not be based solely upon flat-rate entitlements or access through years of contributions.

Modernity 2 and the Re-commodification of Retirement

Since the 1970s, pension funds have become the dominant form of capital investment throughout the global economy. In 2000, 'the total amount of pension savings exceeded the combined capitalisation of the stock markets of London, New York and Tokyo' (Engelen 2003). Relatively unimportant sources of institutional investment in the pre- and post-war era, pension funds have become important as the attractiveness of occupational and personal pensions has grown and as the pension package became incorporated into the wage-bargaining negotiations of the trades unions (Minns 2000). Since the late 1960s, billions of pounds have entered these funds each year, giving the pension fund managers (but not the 'owners' or 'contributors' to the fund) greater power to operate within global financial markets. According to Minns, pension fund growth was one of the principal reasons for the continuing rise in share value during the 1990s, as funds chased short-term investment opportunities. For a long time, pension funds drew in more money than they had to pay out as growing numbers of workers contributed record amounts in line with their rising affluence. A point of equilibrium potentially emerges as the size of the cohorts of workers retiring starts to exceed the size of the cohorts joining the work-force. This may not matter because of the size of the pension funds, but it does pose a threat to the long-term stability of the pension funds themselves.

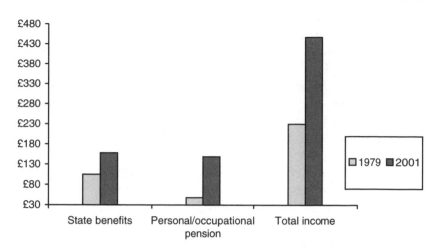

Figure 3.2   Changes in income by source for recently retired UK couples, 1979–2001. Source: Department of Work and Pensions, Pensions Analysts Division 2003: tables 2 and A2.

The post-war welfare state helped to equalize the living standards of older people to a degree that was unknown to many of those retiring during their working lives. The limitation of this 'modest equality', as Esping-Andersen has pointed out, is that 'the poor rely upon the state and the remainder on the market' (Esping-Andersen 1990: 25). This growing reliance upon the market, particularly in those countries where a significant part of the retirement income package comes from private and/or occupational pensions (Australia, Britain, Canada, Holland, New Zealand and the USA), has seen the retirement incomes of dual pension holders rise as a result. Figure 3.2, drawn from the 2002/3 UK pensioner income series, illustrates both the overall rise in retirement income and its changing composition for the period from 1979 through to 2001.

Private sources of income have risen because of the widening population base contributing to occupational/personal pensions and because of rising wages and increased employee contributions. While the working population has begun to experience a slower rate of growth in its income over this latter period, rates of income growth for people in retirement have been maintained. In Britain and in other countries dominated by such multi-pillared pension systems, the effect has been to maintain or even amplify income inequalities in later life. The result is a growing redistribution of income across the lifespan and a reduction in income differentials between those who are still at work and those who are retired. The retired population has become more differentiated within itself, as it has become less differentiated from the working population. This process has gradually eroded pensioners' position as members of a unitary, free-floating de-commodified class. Instead, retirement is reconstituted through a multiplicity of positions each of which provides opportunities for (as well as obstacles to) a continuing, increasingly individualized engagement with the market (i.e. a process of re-commodification).

Summarizing our position so far, we have argued that later life in pre- and early industrial society was constituted as a residual social category whose identity was determined by the inability to earn one's living. The majority of older people who continued to work maintained their position within the productive system, and their lives differed little from those of labouring people of all ages. As industrialization and urbanization became more widespread, old age became a period of life that was increasingly defined by the risk of pauperization, a risk that needed to be insured against much in the same way that workers needed illness and disability insurance. As the probability of reaching and living on in later life increased, the costs of poor relief grew. The various collective provisions made against such an eventuality were gradually taken over by the state, which transformed the status of the unemployed aged from pauper to pensioner.

With the development of the post-war welfare state, old age was more successfully distanced from its status as 'a welfare class', and pensioners began to acquire a position that was relatively protected from the untrammelled workings of the market. What this meant for the majority of people was that later life effectively became a period of reduced income with a guaranteed, if limited, protection against poverty. The modern welfare state sought thus to de-commodify old age, establishing what we termed a free floating class of retirees who were able to enjoy a secure period at the end of their lives. For a 'glorious' thirty-year period after the Second World War, such a reality seemed close to being actualized. From the 1950s through to the 1970s, poorer pensioners saw their incomes rise faster, and the richer saw theirs rise more slowly than had ever been the case in their working lives. For the majority of older people, retirement was a distinct improvement over the inequality that had dogged their earlier working lives. But it remained a 'modest equality' insufficient to meet the aspirations of subsequent generations of middle- and working-class people as they themselves grew older. The turn to 'the market' has effectively re-commodified retirement. Although this process of re-commodification has been most marked in Anglo-Saxon countries, the steady growth in multi-pillar retirement income packages has extended the process to countries which traditionally have been models of de-commodification such as Sweden and Denmark. Inequalities within the working population are matched or even outpaced by inequalities in later life, as the boundaries between the re-commodification and de-commodification of later life have become harder to define.

Retirement, Power and Class: What Is Different About Modernity 2?

Starting with the affluence that has spread throughout the whole class structure of industrialized nations since the second half of the twentieth century allows us to situate this re-commodification of later life. This affluence has caused problems for many theorists of class, as they implicitly base their approach on the existence of a simple relationship between class and poverty. While these complex debates need not concern us here, we can borrow some of the insights promoted by them to better our understanding of the transformation and fragmentation of the social categorization of later life. We can draw upon one recent formulation provided by Graham Scambler's triad of Logics, Relations and Figurations to show how later life is being reconfigured by (and itself helps reconfigure) issues of class and power (Scambler 2002). Scambler's argument, developed primarily in relation to the debate over health inequalities, is that we need to see the processes operating on social class as continually chang-

ing. One set of figurations does not have to be taken as representative of all. The poverty that characterized later life at the start
of the twentieth century does not have to be the dominant facet
of later life at the start of the twenty-first century. We also need
to recognize the constant logic of capitalist relations that deter-
mines a continuing power differential in the ability to obtain
material and social advantage. It is this power differential that
creates and re-creates the conflicts around class. The fact that
social class figurations change does not mean that the logic underlying class ceases to operate as a social structuring process.

As we have already noted, the post-war expansion of finance
capitalism has been fuelled by a massive growth in investment
funds, capital formed largely from the cumulative savings of insurance, pensions and other personal finance schemes. The declining
profits of traditional industry and the diminishing role of the individual investor have been more than offset by these new capital
formations, which now exceed those of all other sources of capital
investment. Because of the preponderance of pension funds
amongst these institutional investors, the term 'grey capitalism',
coined by Robin Blackburn, is particularly apt. While the need 'to
speculate to accumulate' remains, the forms of speculation and
the mechanisms for speculation have expanded in parallel with
the growth of the institutional investor. The consequences for the
relationship between markets and pensions have already been
commented upon:

> Public investors in the mutual fund, whether they understand the
> workings of the arrangement or not, are bound into a set of money
> forms that are dependent on calculating future times and spaces;
> that is, what is going to happen, say, to Japanese inflation rates and
> general economic performance in twelve months time. *The future
> performance of distant spaces* is thus destined to become part of the
> present of, in this case, US pensioners. The pace and rhythm of
> global finance is thus transferred into the everyday through the
> abstract qualities of these new forms of money. (Pryke and Allen
> 2000: 273)

As Minns has argued, the high returns initially available made
private pensions particularly attractive to national political elites

eager to cut back on their responsibilities. The relations that emerged from these logics represented a break with the past, a transformation of the social compact that now stressed the importance of personal choice, whether in the expression of identity or in the safeguarding of risk. A reliance on the benefits of citizenship rights became one of several differentiated outcomes arising from each individual's personal situation. Individuals needed to invest both in pensions and in good jobs to be assured of the resources in later life to maintain their identity and their lifestyle. Work, leisure, home/work balance and retirement were presented as matters of individual choice. Even the failure to choose has become a choice. While this movement into Modernity 2 was led by the Anglo-Saxon regimes of the Reagan–Thatcher axis, the process has filtered through to other more 'corporatist' states as the underlying stability upon which they were presaged was undermined by the need to integrate with a global and, seemingly more open, economy.

What is clear, however, is that at the dawn of the twenty-first century there is no sign of a revived Beveridgian welfare state model waiting in the wings to be unveiled. Within the liberal welfare state, privatization and individualization of retirement income have become the order of the day, with the role of the state confined to assuring a 'minimum income guarantee' (Brooks, Regan and Robinson 2002: 36). Pressures on corporate welfare states to follow a similar path have been more or less resisted, but at the cost of preserving many of the economic inequalities of working life.

Those in positions of control inevitably seek to ensure the advantages of their position by negotiating various protective 'options' for their own personal retirement, and access to the 'surplus' is still unevenly distributed (Haseler 2000). Despite the greater opportunities for those in control of capital to secure a satisfactorily de-commodified retirement, choice still remains the cultural leitmotif of Modernity 2 and has an effect upon them. Choice demands that the clerk as well as the CEO, the foreman as well as the fund manager, behave as if they are equally free to choose how best to fund their later life. In conditions of shared uncertainty, albeit with differing resources to manage it, each actor is deemed responsible for his or her outcome. While the state offers assistance, guidance and counsel, increasingly it seeks to keep itself out of the ring.

As pension funds grow in significance, a key question is whether pensioners are becoming latter-day *rentiers* whose income is dependent on the profits made by younger generations. Does the process of re-commodifying retirement through a growing engagement with 'personal financial management' create a more ambiguous set of class relations in later life? Some have argued that the lines of fracture lie, not between the controllers of and the contributors to private or occupational pension funds, but between the interests of those who are beginning employment and those who have ceased to labour. This is not simply a conflict of interests between people at different points of the lifecourse, but also reflects the idea that the returns from labour constitute 'property rights', a view that may be shared by beneficiaries of funded and PAYGO systems alike.

Issues of control and access to the surplus underlie the differential fates of state pensioners, the holders of occupational pensions, and those who are in receipt of private pensions. Conflicts emerge when returns are not what were expected, whether through the downsizing of citizenship benefits, the re-calibration of PAYGO entitlements, the uncertainties of corporate assets, or the failures of financial markets. Occupational pension holders are at risk of scheme failures as employers' past pensions holidays make their impact, or, as in the case of companies such as Enron, when corporate failure wreaks devastation. These potential crises over funded and unfunded pensions create further sites of conflict. While some are based upon traditional class relations, others draw upon gender and generational differences and the contrasting position of those in the public and private sectors of the economy.

Those countries attempting to reform the benefits provided by national social insurance systems are equally witness to the new lines of fracture created by financial globalization. The 'continental' European welfare states have made the least alteration to their system of social insurance contributions and benefits. This reflects particular figurations in the relationship between national capital, labour and the state, which are more nationally integrated than in liberal welfare states. This is evident in their political make-up and decision making. The result is an institutionalized resistance to system reform. Most corporate welfare systems of social insurance preserve more than they equalize the conditions of working life in retirement, thereby creating the idea that pensions are a form of 'sacrosanct' property rights. Although the tensions associated with protecting income in retirement exist in all the advanced economies, the structural capacity to resolve those tensions through resisting neo-liberal solutions varies (Swank 2002). The competing interests of a globally oriented capitalism and a nationally orientated population of retirees or potential retirees reflect the broader conflict between international and national capitals. This paradox equally affects the one remaining superpower. Niall Ferguson (2004) has argued that the need to maintain the incomes of older Americans is one of the reasons limiting and ultimately undermining US global power:

> Americans like security. But they like Social Security more than national security. It is their preoccupation with the hazards of old age and ill health that will prove to be the real cause of their country's fiscal overstretch, not their preoccupation with the hazards of terrorism and the 'axis of evil'. (Ferguson 2004: 269)

While the situation of the USA may be unique by its being both a major national economy and a foundation of the global economy, it is fair to say that the nation-state in addressing the needs of one can end up in conflict with the other. The relative levels of elite integration into either national or global capital serves, then, as a critical variable in the articulation of power.

In Modernity 2, the interrelationships between working and post-working life have established *new* sites of inequality. Whereas in Modernity 1, the principal site for these conflicts was between a national working class and a national bourgeoisie, a conflict that found its resolution in the modern welfare state, in Modernity 2, the sites of conflict have multiplied, and their resolution no longer appears to lie in the national compacts of the past. Nor does their resolution lie with corporate finance. To quote Gordon Clark, 'no public or private institutions (including the nation state and large corporations) can now guarantee the final benefit of pension benefits' (Clark 2003: 1339). The way in which later life connects with the social relations of class is no longer reducible to the political economy of the nation-state. The various figurations of pension entitlements that emerged from the particular histories of individual states are becoming internationalized. Financial globalization affects all levels of society and operates across both public and private sectors of the economy. Increasingly, the financial resources tied up in funding later life are becoming central to the functioning of the world economy, and the vicissitudes of the world economy, correspondingly, are of growing significance to the fate of all retirees.

Conclusion

The argument that we have presented in this chapter is that the twentieth century has seen the rise and fall of the notion that the old could be defined *en masse* as a 'de-commodified' pensioner population. Through a variety of differing means, the retired population has become a more complex and socially differentiated group within society. In Modernity 2, the economic circumstances of all age-groups before, during and after working life are equally complex and equally difficult to reduce to any single structure of 'dependency'. This has been a result of the success of post-war European societies and their social policies in de-commodifying the lifecourse. But this is only one part of the story. Later life is no longer a site of conflict because of its endemic poverty. There is poverty in later life, but poverty is not its defining condition. Rather, the contemporary crisis is over a new image of later life, a crisis of meaning that is exemplified in and by the third age. Establishing and maintaining a comfortable income in later life is now the major consideration affecting not just those in retirement but also younger cohorts of working adults struggling to maintain the prospect of a third age in their own lifetimes.

Examining the circumstances in which the economic basis for later life is funded helps to clarify the linkages between class, power and later life and identifies some of the sites of conflict around the third age. The cultural significance of consumerism affects all age-groups and all social classes. The desire and expectation of people to continue to be included in this culture before, during and after their working life ends explains why the arguments for good post-work incomes are so acute. Stimulation of consumption is not intended to liberate people from their ties with the market; rather, it maintains them and thereby helps maintain the reproduction of capital. As markets expand and mass consumption moves beyond the reproduction of mass labour, the figurations of capitalist relations change. Time freed from the necessity of labour increases. The conflict over where the money will come from to sustain this new 'surplus' continues the argument between capital and labour. Class is but one site of this conflict. Other sites have emerged, between the interests of global and national capital, between the lifecourses of men and women, between economic prosperity and social legitimation, and between the moral responsibilities of the state and the moral responsibilities of its citizens. The issue of inequality in later life is important *per se*, but it is the changing contexts affecting the (social) nature of later life that are, and we would argue should remain, of principle concern for the contemporary study of ageing.

4

Cohort and Generation and the Study of Social Change

Sociology and the social sciences generally have paid less attention to the horizontal divisions within society (cohort, age-group) than they have to its vertical divisions (class and gender). Perhaps this is because the latter divisions existed in such stark form when these disciplines were developing. As modernity has become more reflexively periodized, horizontal divisions within society have gained in salience. A new approach to the study of social change is emerging which proposes that generation is replacing class as the key site of contemporary social conflict (Turner 1989; Becker 1991). Given this refocusing of interests, there is clearly a need to develop a more coherent interpretation of concepts such as 'life stage', 'cohort', 'period' and 'generation'.

Attempts to understand the role of time in the lives of individuals, groups and communities are plagued with difficulties. Nowhere is the conflict between agency and structure, 'sociology's defining problematic', more acutely felt than in the attempt to analyse the relationship between the lives of individuals and the times they live in – between history and biography (Hardy and Waite 1997: 2). Two approaches dominate the conceptualization of this problem. The first emphasizes the cultural distinctiveness of generations. This is the approach associated particularly with Karl Mannheim. In his seminal paper on the 'problem of generations' Mannheim wrote that the term 'generation' contained two related and essential elements (Mannheim 1952/1997). The first refers to a common location in historical time (generational location), the second to a distinct consciousness of that historical position, a 'mentalité' or 'entelechie' formed by the events and experiences of that time (generational style). Both location and consciousness are necessary elements, in Mannheim's formulation, in order that 'generation' can function as a structuring process on a par with the vertical structures of class and gender.

The second approach is associated with the demographer Norman Ryder. He argued that generational location is better represented through the more neutral construct 'cohort', which he defined as 'that aggregate of individuals who experienced the same event within the same time interval . . . [where typically] the defining event has been birth' (Ryder 1965/1997: 68). For Ryder, cohort represents 'a proxy measure for what are in fact traits, dispositions and behaviours and . . . the social relationships in which [they] are embedded, that actually carry the "effect" and provide theoretically meaningful interpretation' (Hardy and Waite 1997: 6). By excluding Mannheim's second component, generational style or consciousness, Ryder emptied the idea of cohort of any endogenous (some might say 'mythical') significance it may seem to possess as a vehicle of social change. He wanted to treat 'generation' as a form of social categorization whose explanatory power derives primarily, if not exclusively, from its role as a 'surrogate ind[ex] for the common experiences of many people in each category' (Ryder 1965/1997: 72). Seeking to bring methodological clarity to the study of social change, Ryder argued that cohort should serve as the lens through which other more deterministic processes of social change can be observed. Whilst helping to focus attention on the distinct experiences of a particular generation, 'cohort' remained, for Ryder, an analytic tool to uncover processes whose understanding lay elsewhere.

The proposal to shed the 'spirit of hermeneutics' (Kohli 1996: 2) that seemed to be embedded in Mannheim's position did not lead to any resolution of the problem of generation. Kertzer has argued that Mannheim's difficulty was confounding the genealogical meaning of generation (the link between parents and children) with two other distinct phenomena: namely, cohort (a population sharing a common historical origin, typically a shared year of birth) and historical period or era (a common set of historically determinate experiences (Kertzer 1983)). The solution for Kertzer, as for Ryder before him, was to confine the term 'generation' strictly to its usage as a term for parent/child relationships and to use 'cohort' to represent a population sharing a common historical experience by virtue of sharing a common year of birth. These and many similar injunctions have fallen on deaf ears. The contemporary use of the term 'generation' retains its allegorical linkage with systems of intra-familial transmission and the re-production of the domestic household. It also retains the sense of a shared historical consciousness, so central to the experience of continuity and change in modernity, and, of course, it frequently substitutes for 'cohort'. Despite its 'waffly' status (P. Abrams 1970), the Mannheimian concept of generation has persisted within the social sciences. It possesses a resonance that cannot be easily ignored.

The term 'cohort' also is not without its own problems. How does one determine the boundaries of 'a common date of birth'? And when exactly does one cohort begin and another one end? As with 'generation', this term cannot be returned to its original meaning, and a degree of arbitrariness cannot be avoided when defining who or what constitutes a cohort. This is true for any, if not all attempts at periodization. However insistent a reality in human life, time cannot be other than a social construction, the significance of which will vary between societies and at different points in the history of those societies. Even within the same society at a particular period in history, different groups will assign different meanings to 'their' time. Consider the conflict between the early factory-owners and their workers over the latter's resis-tance to factory discipline, manifested in their reluctance to come in to work on 'Saint Mondays' (Thompson 1993: 337–8).

Accepting such caveats, it is widely recognized that time in all its various manifestations has become of increasing importance in structuring life experiences (Harvey 1989; Bergman 1992). From the slower cyclical rhythms of traditional societies to the multi-plicity of time zones and time references within Modernity 2, time has become an inescapable reference point for organizing our daily lives. Individual and collective consciousness of time forms essen-tial components in contemporary social identities. Age conscious-ness and consciousness of the temporal specificity of many of the products and practices of contemporary life have become more acute. Despite this, the study of time in all its social manifesta-tions – whether as age, cohort or period – remains an under-researched and under-theorized area (Corsten 1999).

The earliest concerns of writers such as Comte, Durkheim and Marx focused upon historical periodization rather than upon age or cohort. For them, there was only one really important 'transition' or 'era': namely, the emergence of modern urban industrial society. The notion of a society undergoing 'revolutions' in its social relations and systems of symbolic exchange began to be articulated from the latter half of the nineteenth century. This focus upon change, however, concentrated primarily upon the origins of 'modern society'. During the twentieth century the focus changed, and the time frame shortened. Change was to be reckoned more in decades than centuries. The greater differentiation of culture by cohort experiences (the multiplication of generational units, to use Mannheim's terminology) and the compression of generational time into ever narrower periodizations lead to a greater segmentation of modernity. The sensitivity to and desire for change that was expressed in the arrival of 'modernism' as a cultural moment has become ever more intense. The influence of class and neighbourhood as 'enculturing' institutions has diminished correspondingly. The hyper-differentiation (individualization) of post-war welfare societies (Beck and Beck-Gernsheim 2001; Leisering and Leibfried 1999) and the turn toward a politics based upon recognition and identity (Fraser 1995) have problematized the nature of self, both as regards to its extension over time (the problem of a stable self) as well as its location within time (the problem of the temporal contingencies of collective identities).

By the late 1960s, generational lifestyles, capable of enduring 'beyond the bounds of age spans, age groups and, in principle, the life cycle', were seen as having replaced, or being about to replace previous forms of social insertion (P. Abrams 1970: 183). When Philip Abrams made this suggestion, he nevertheless assumed that these new generational lifestyles would be presaged upon a shared political world-view, albeit fashioned by a distinct 'post-war' outlook. Others proposed similar broad changes in generational world-views based upon the full realization of modernity as society moved from conditions of scarcity to those of a new post-scarcity. Inglehart, for example, sought to demonstrate the existence of an inter-generational shift in values. He saw this shift as representing a move from those concerned with, and fashioned by, the need for material security that preoccupied cohorts born before the Depression of the 1930s, to 'post-materialist' issues, such as personal liberty and self-expression, that have preoccupied cohorts born since (Inglehart 1997). Others have emphasized the mass expansion of 'surplus' or 'decorative' consumption as a key source of generational differentiation that was first epitomized in the lifestyle youth movements of the 1960s (Murdock and McCron 1976; Hebdige 1979). Given the many sources that can serve as a base for what Mannheim had called 'generational consciousness', the principal question that this chapter addresses is how 'generation' should best be understood. This question, we shall argue, can only be addressed by considering how historical periods are expressed and realized within individual lifecourses, for it is through the interaction between cohorts and periods that generations emerge.

The Limits and Boundaries of a Generation

Raymond Williams has argued that 'the modern sense of generation in the . . . sense of a distinctive kind of people or attitudes . . . only fully develop[ed] from the mid-nineteenth century' (Williams 1983: 140). According to Williams, the new cultural and intellectual sensibilities that began to emerge during this time fostered a progressive, developmental approach to history, which became the study of how society was moving toward the realization of a socially progressive future. 'Generation' was imbued with an added significance as being both the 'carrier' of and the 'arena' where these new cultures established themselves. Consciousness of generation went hand in hand with consciousness of humanity's capacity for social revolution. For Williams, 1848 was a watershed. After the revolutionary events of that year, 'generation' could no longer 'unthink itself' back to a mere cyclical biological process. It had achieved a 'conscience collective', and thereby become a potential social and political institution.

'Generational cohort analysis' has flourished most within the field of 'political' sociology (Cutler 1977). Here the approach has been to draw boundaries around birth cohort groups and link these boundaries to external events in order to examine secular changes in socio-political attitudes. Writers have varied in the extent to which they have emphasized each cohort's generational location (Cutler 1977) or its shared consciousness (Schuman and Scott 1989). Only amongst the latter group of researchers has serious thought been given to identifying the boundaries of a 'generational style'. Harrison White has argued that 'cohorts only become [social] actors when they cohere enough around events . . . to be called generations' (White 1992: 31). He defines generation as 'a joint interpretive construction which insists upon and builds among tangible cohorts defining a style recognized from outside as well as from inside itself' (White 1992: 31). White argues that generation is a cohort's consciousness of itself – conscious of what it is and how it differs from other cohorts. By drawing attention to this consciousness of difference, White raises, though does not solve, the issue of boundaries, as well as the means by which generational or cohort boundaries can be constructed.

Michael Corsten has also addressed this problem. In response to 'the problem of the historical constitution of generations as collective identities' (Corsten 1999: 250), Corsten suggests that generations acquire a sense of collective identity within 'cultural circles', which he defines as common and distinct forms of discourse and social practice. The concept of 'cultural circles' has a potential heuristic value, but Corsten fails to give it real purchase by leaving open the question of how any generation goes about articulating its generational consciousness and how a generation forms its cultural circles. For there to be a generational consciousness (or identity or lifestyle, the issue remains the same), there need to be events or practices located in time that shape the discourses that set the boundaries of the generational field.

Most research has focused upon public events. Henk Becker (1991) has tried to develop empirical tests of generational boundaries through his examination of Dutch social change in the post-war era. Like Corsten and other supporters of Mannheim's position, Becker argues that 'generation' is taking over from 'social class' as the major dynamic of social change in the post-war period. He writes that 'as soon as society moves toward openness, specific generations become institutionalised and partially take over the role of social classes as arrangements for the allocation of opportunities [and] the distribution of scarce goods'. (Becker 1991: 221–2). Exposure to key historical events that take place during each cohort's transition to adulthood provides the markers for each generational field. Becker argues that there have been five key 'events' which have defined the generational identities of post-war cohorts in Dutch society: the Depression, the Second World War, the post-war labour boom, the 'cultural revolution of the 1960s', and the Seventies 'recession'. Birth cohorts growing up within each of these periods have been shaped into a generation by the unique influence of these events. Becker acknowledges, but gives less significance to, processes of continuous change, such as expanding educational provision, developments in the labour market, and the transformation of the position of women.

A major problem with Becker's approach is that he equates specific historical events with social changes that extend beyond the events themselves and are not contained by them. The collective identity of a generation, one that is actively felt and articulated by members of that generation, and one which structures their actions as social agents, cannot be generated by borrowing from history and ascribing from that an identity. A better definition of a generation's 'cultural circle' is needed than one based simply upon living through particular historical events. By focusing upon selected socio-political events as Becker, White and others have done, an appearance of precision is established which places the onus upon the 'event' or 'period' to confer an 'identity-generating' meaning. The translation of a historical event into the collective identity of a generation is then given a determining role in social change. One could just as easily omit the central term. What happens then is social history, not sociology.

Although the approach of writers such as Ryder (1965/1997) and Kertzer (1983) appears empirically more exacting, in explicitly avoiding any ascription of collective agency to a birth cohort, the advocates of a cohort approach face the same boundary problems over the width or narrowness of a birth cohort. Nevertheless, treating cohort as a social lens allows for a focus on the processes of social change themselves. If the advocates of a generational approach, such as Becker (2000) and Edmunds and Turner

(2002), are to advance their case, they must define the nature of generational identities and the means by which they function as structuring influences in ways that move beyond privileging 'critical events'. Cultural identities may incorporate historical events in defining a shared history, as Benedict Anderson (1991) has argued in his account of the imagined community of the nation. However, such signifiers are typically established retrospectively, and their relationship to present social realities is iconic rather than experientially formative in the way that students of political generations seem to claim (Cutler 1977).

Generational Identities and the Cultural Turn

Attempts at empirical pattern analysis based upon the juxtaposition of certain birth cohorts with certain historical events do not provide a satisfactory delineation of a 'generation-cohort' as a social identity, let alone as a potential structuring structure. What other methodologies might? Much of the work seeking to provide an empirical delineation of 'generation' has come from political sociology. An alternative approach is that drawn from cultural studies, with its emphasis upon ideas of 'identity' and 'difference'. Distinct events and episodes in history impinge upon individual lives in many complex ways, not least through the media by which those events reach the individual, and whose interpretations of the events provide a cultural or symbolic frame of reference. As local communities have declined in significance, shared access to and shared meanings of public events are increasingly provided by public media whose market audiences may be much broader than a local or even a national community. The virtual communities established by the media (radio, TV and the Internet) can be thought of as the cultural circles that Corsten (1999) suggests shape generational consciousness.

By shifting attention from political sociology to cultural studies, alternative approaches to conceptualizing 'generation' become possible. Generation then becomes not so much an aggregate of individuals born at a certain time as a cultural field emerging at a particular moment in history. Such a cultural field shapes and is shaped by the particular tastes, values and dispositions of some cohorts more comprehensively than it does others. It is a short step to integrate this insight with the work of the cultural sociologist Pierre Bourdieu. Corsten's suggestive reference to the role of 'cultural circles' (Corsten 1999: 261–2) in defining the boundaries of a generation can be re-defined by making use of Bourdieu's conceptualizations of 'habitus' and 'field'.[1] Mannheim's concept of a generational location can be equally re-defined as a generational 'field', one characterized by the emergence of a changed relationship between past and present social spaces. Generational style or consciousness can be treated, in like fashion, as a generational 'habitus' – a set of dispositions that generate and structure individual practices, which emerge and are defined by the forces operating within a particular generational field. Such an interpretation accords well with Bourdieu's own work on 'generations', when he stated that:

> generational conflicts oppose not age classes separated by natural properties but habitus which have been produced by different modes of generation . . . which . . . cause one group to experience as natural and reasonable practices or aspirations which another group finds unthinkable or scandalous. (Bourdieu 1977: 78)

As Bourdieu points out, habitus are not the expressions of 'any intentional calculation or conscious reference to a norm' but the products of a 'systematicity' within the objective circumstances surrounding a social group or class which are 'laid down in each agent by his earliest upbringing' (Bourdieu 1977: 80–1). In other words, it is the links that exist within the discourse and practices of a particular group that reveals the habitus, rather than the individuals' reflections upon their actions. Habitus are thus derived from, but are not defined by, the distinctive actions of particular people in particular settings or fields.

To elaborate our earlier distinction between 'generation' and 'cohort', the former represents a distinct, temporally located cultural field within which individuals from a variety of overlapping birth cohorts participate as generational agents. This needs to be distinguished from a conceptualization based on the exposure of a particular aggregate of individuals to a specific event or set of 'socializing' events. Greater or lesser 'access' to that cultural field distinguishes each cohort. The degree and nature of participation will structure the depth and breadth of the habitus that a particular cohort and hence age-group form.

The advantages of formulating 'the problem of generation' in this way are threefold. First, it avoids the well-recognized problem of the overdetermined identity between age-groups, cohorts and periods, whereby each is defined as the product of the other two (see Mason et al. 1973). Because each term is treated as being constituted out of the other two, no distinct explanations can be made for one element without it being equally determinate for the others. Treating generation as a cultural field avoids defining it by reference to membership of a specific cohort. Secondly, such an approach enables actors to be treated as individuals who will inevitably vary in their level of engagement with emerging and established generational fields. Each individual member of a birth cohort need not serve as a 'representative' of this or that generation. Thirdly, this approach recognizes the importance of changing material conditions that structure the symbolic exchange that mediates such patterns of engagement, enabling a focus upon the engines that create the new circuits of cultural capital.

To illustrate this approach in a more concrete fashion, we shall explore the establishment of modern 'youth culture' which emerged in the post-Second World War period at the time when Modernity 1 was reaching its apotheosis. This choice is guided by a more general argument, which we shall elaborate further in the next chapter: namely, that the third age can best be conceptualized as the elaboration of an existent generational field that was first established within post-war 'youth culture'. We shall argue that the significance of this generational field lay less in its youth than in its role in realizing a society permeated by mass consumption. The confounding of the 'decorative' aspects of youth culture (Hebdidge 1979), with the more substantive shift toward consumption that was taking place at that time has led many to equate life stage with consumption. The result is that 'youthfulness' has become associated with consumption, and 'age' with the failure to participate in consumer culture. This association is one that we sought to unravel in the first chapter. It is now the place to explore what established the association in the first place.

Post-War Youth Culture as 'Generational Field'

That which once constituted 'youth culture' as a distinct generational field is now no longer confined (if it ever was) to the practices of people of a particular age. But the origins of this particular
generational field refer to circumstances and experiences that
specifically affected the youth of a particular era. Its distinctiveness lies in the centrality of age in forming its initial boundaries.
Youth culture was a clearly defined set of practices that engaged
teenagers and young men and women at all levels of society. It
privileged practices that were dependent upon, but not confined
within, the expanding fields of retail capital. As Capuzzo has
pointed out, 'young people as a uniform category without significant internal differences reappeared in the . . . 1950s . . . as the
product of an attempt to build a new market – in other words, a
commercial and media creation' (Capuzzo 2001: 156). But it was
more than merely a commercial and media creation, it was a field
in which young people themselves exercised a growing influence.
It was the systemic interrelationships between the actions, discourse and consumption of young people that helped found the
generational field that would later situate the third age for those
growing up in this period.

As these interrelationships grew more extensive, they incorporated a wider range of products and practices. The idea of 'lifestyle'
began to expand beyond the various youth subcultures in which
it had first been consciously realized to encompass other age-
groups, both younger and older than themselves. The boundaries of
the generational field that originally constituted 'youth culture'
grew progressively looser, just as attempts to re-create 'new' and
'distinct' youth cultures imploded. The heritage we now possess
is a post-generational culture whose origins lie in the youth
culture of that period, but whose boundaries have been progressively subverted. As the market pursues a relentless programme
of consumer segmentation to maintain its centrality as the dominant source of social differentiation, 'youthfulness' now extends
across the lifecourse, whilst the social stratification of time is fragmented into ever smaller micro-generational moments. Years
replace decades as potential 'generational units', rendering the

'stages of life' less solid points of reference from which to sustain a mass culture. A trans-generational habitus has emerged as cohort after cohort is socialized into the processes and practices of re-creational consumption. The effect has been to render increasingly permeable the lifecourse divisions established by Modernity 1. Children, adolescents, adults of working age and retired people have all gained access to a common post-generational habitus. People of all ages share similar, consumerist preoccupations with food and diet, fitness and health, lifestyle and leisure. The 'playful' use of cosmetics, the undifferentiated presence of pop music, the ubiquitous holidays abroad, as well as the tendency to treat shopping as leisure and leisure as 'work', induces people of differing ages to identify themselves as less differentiated citizen consumers sharing in a largely age-denying popular culture.

A UK time–use survey, conducted in 2000, revealed that what most people do as 'leisure', when they are not sleeping, working or doing housework, engaged in child care, eating, drinking, resting or socializing is remarkably similar. Despite some degree of variation in the time spent watching TV, it is important to recognize how similar leisure activities are across age-groups (table 4.1). The media helped create the code and communicate the new generational field, and the media continue to play a key role in sustaining it, not least through their domination of people's leisure time.

The interlinking cultural worlds of the mass media and the advertising, entertainment and fashion industries established an aestheticization of everyday life. Together with the general expansion of markets and the increased availability of credit, this created a new set of 'objective conditions' for the elaboration of a generational field whose boundaries were no longer organized by the division of labour and the controls of established capital. The pre-war generational field had grown old. The inter-generational solidarities of class and community, the oppressive uniformity of working life, and the limited pursuits of leisure suddenly appeared as dated elements of a European past that the war and its immediate aftermath had discredited. Cut off emotionally from that past and galvanized by the Americanization of European culture, a new cohort of would-be citizens began to articulate and exercise a new vision for Europe. Within the context of more integrated and more materially secure nation-states, these new voices

Table 4.1   Average time (in minutes) spent in Britain each day on different 'leisure' activities by age-group: 2000

Leisure time activity	8–15 yrs	16–24 yrs	25–44 yrs	45–64 yrs	65+ yrs
Entertainment and culture	9	8	7	6	5
Sport and outdoor activities	29	20	14	15	14
Reading	10	10	16	32	58
Watching TV/video	139	141	129	145	196
Listening to music and radio	8	11	5	6	13
Travel	76	96	94	85	58
As percentage of day	19	20	18	20	24

Source: Data derived from <www.statistics.gov.uk/statbase/Expodata/Spread sheets/D7038.xls>. Time spent on main activity by age-group: UK Time Use Survey (Office of National Statistics 2004).

helped shape a cultural revolution whose resonance has continued to affect the lives of each succeeding birth cohort growing up in the latter half of the twentieth century. The maturation of this post-war youth culture has set the conditions for a pervasive and destabilizing consumerist habitus that dominates the post-generational culture of Modernity 2.

The Ageing of Youth Culture or the Maturing of Consumer Society?

What implications does this analysis have for the study of the social and cultural determinants of later life? While youth may possess universal qualities, youth culture is much more contingent. During the 1950s and 1960s in America and in Europe, 'a largely novel phenomenon' emerged, the universal valuing of 'the autonomous working-class teen'. In America, this image seemed to subvert the ideals of an aspiring middle-class consumer citizen, threatening to break the bond between earning the right to leisure and by earning a decent living. In Europe, the transformation of the working-class teenager took a little longer to be established. But when it finally came, in the 1960s, it heralded the end of a historic working-class culture that, in different ways and in different countries, had valorized the working man as honest breadwinner and his counterpart, the industrious working-class matriarch, as the force that held the family together. The generational break between the 'habitus' of working-class youth and those of their parents was one of the central features of the Sixties' cultural revolution, a revolution that changed the destiny of the working class from that of an economic to a culturally 'universal' class.

'Youth culture' and 'mass consumer society' share a common origin. But age itself was less the fundamental divide that it was claimed to be. The democratization of the lifecourse had begun long before, when in 1948 *Time* magazine announced that the US population had increased by 2,800,000 more 'consumers' (Hine 2000: 250). Working through the logic of a mass consumer society takes time. The universal 'youth culture' that emerged in the 1950s was a phenomenon created by US advertisers at the same time as being a 'counter-cultural' reaction to the materialism of those who cut their teeth during the Depression (Hine 2000: 237–8). By attributing to the 'older' generation the fossilized distinctions between 'popular' and 'high' culture, it was possible to agitate for a cultural revolution that pitted, not working-class interests against middle-class interests, but the universal desire of youth against the particularities of age.

Once a victory of sorts had been established for youth culture as the universal vanguard of the new mass culture, scope for further cultural revolution became more limited. The vectors of that generational divide had been determined. All that subsequent birth cohorts could do was to follow and elaborate them. As those generational warriors are growing older, taking with them much of the kudos and the more significant spoils of victory, further generational divisions are less easy to establish, and even when established, less easy to sustain. The question of what constituted that youth culture is, in retrospect, difficult to answer. Does it define a particular historical period? Can or should it be distinguished from a 'youthful' period in the development of mass consumer society? As the material symbols of what was once portrayed as the 'youth revolution' fade, and the individual icons of that period age, do they still function as the boundaries of a cultural field that was so age- (youth-) defined. Perhaps those things that were once taken as representative of youth were really the symbols of a new stage in social relations, one that valorized authenticity over authority, consumption over production, novelty over familiarity, and partnership over parenthood. Defined not so much as an age-group but as the product of a 'new' generational field, the third age is the continuing manifestation (or maturation) of what once was called 'youth' culture. Rather than treating the third age as a particular 'lucky' cohort, it makes more sense to treat it as the cultural expression of a generational field that, born in Modernity 1, has reached maturity within Modernity 2.

5

Later Life and the
Two Generational Fields
of Modernity

In the last chapter we argued that many of the differences between age-groups can be understood as the result of differential rates of participation by members of differing birth cohorts in distinct 'generational fields'. The aim of this chapter is to pursue our argument by exploring the two generational fields that dominated the twentieth century. The transition from the generational field of Modernity 1 to the generational field of Modernity 2 forms the nexus from which the 'third age' has arisen. That transition is beginning to exercise a commanding influence over the lives of retired people in contemporary Western societies. It is an influence whose effects cannot be reversed.

The first generational field of Modernity 1 dominated the lives of those born at the end of the nineteenth and early twentieth centuries. It provided continuity between the lives of youth, adults and older people right up to the 1960s. The 1960s were the watershed, marking the break when the second generational field began to emerge. Those growing up after the 1960s are participants in a social and cultural world that has grown distinct from that which was dominant throughout the first half of the twentieth century. The second generational field that began to be established within the youth culture of the post-war period is what is making the experience of later life in the twenty-first century so different from the institutionalized old age that was formed by Modernity 1.

Manual work, limited leisure and pervasive labour market insecurity dominated the lives of most men born into the first generational field. Their working life was disrupted at its start and at its end by major wars. When in the 1950s the men of this generation acquired a secure retirement, there was relatively little time and even less money with which to enjoy the experience. For the majority of women born during this period, marriage, home and children provided much more encompassing experiences than did work. For them, retirement was neither a socially defined nor a personally meaningful event. Its significance lay in accommodating their husband's presence at home and the reduction in household income following retirement.

Men and women from later birth cohorts have begun to experience more similar lives (see e.g. Ortner 2003). They have shared the experience of being teenagers together at secondary school. Although most started work in blue-collar jobs, only a minority will have remained manual workers through to retirement. The majority of men and women will have experienced rising standards of living throughout their working lives, and many will retire from paid employment with either a personal or occupational pension or a substantial earnings-related pension (Yamada 2002). Members of these birth cohorts have had no direct experience of world war, no exposure to mass unemployment; nor have they been faced with extended periods of economic insecurity. The pensioners of the twenty-first century have experienced a life of secure, and continuing cumulative advantage.

The Lifecourse of Modernity 1

Between 1880 and 1960, there was a steady increase in older men's exit from the work-force as retirement emerged as a mass phenomenon. Even so, for most of this period, men in Europe and in the United States continued to work into their sixties and early seventies (Conrad 1990). The threat of unemployment remained a serious problem. It affected working men of all ages, and because the threat accumulated over the lifecourse, it linked together 'retirement' and 'joblessness' (Lee 2003). Like their fathers before them, men worked almost exclusively in settings where their work colleagues were other men (Hakim 1979). They found employment as skilled or unskilled manual workers, and they assumed that their sons would become manual workers, in their turn.[1] Only when they were reaching the end of their lives did they begin to witness their grandchildren moving out in significant numbers from their 'class of origin', in a process of social and cultural change that was unlike anything they or their families had ever before witnessed.[2]

By 1960, less than half the older male population was still working (Conrad 1990). Pensions had become almost universal, and their net replacement value compared with average earnings had risen in Britain, from a base of 18 per cent in 1930 to nearly 30 per cent by 1951. At the same time, there were signs of a drawing apart of the generations. Many of the men returning from active service after the war found themselves set apart from the children who had grown up in their absence. The outline of a generational divide, present as an unrealized potential within this first generational field, would become evident within the new generational field that emerged in the 1960s.

The position for women was not dissimilar. Female employment had increased as a result of the demands of the war economy, but in the immediate post-First World War period there had been a retrenchment. During the 1920s and 1930s, the majority of married women did not go out to work. The separation between work and home remained a highly gendered affair, while age itself played a much less significant part. Wives, daughters, mothers and grandmothers stayed at home; husbands, sons, fathers and grandfathers went out to work. When young women did go out to work, they were employed in low-paid work and continued to 'live at home subject to their parents' rules and regulations, and most of their income went straight to their mothers so they had little financial independence' (E. Roberts 1995: 45).

Once married (and the vast majority did marry), they returned to a position of unwaged domestic labour, supported in their role as wife and mother by their own mothers, whose lives theirs so closely mirrored. For women whose mothers did not live nearby, support was always forthcoming from other women, neighbours, relatives or in-laws. The bond between 'ageing' mothers and their adult daughters remained a central feature of working-class communities until well after the Second World War, though it would become attenuated as women growing up in the second generational field themselves began to reach retirement age toward the end of the twentieth century.

Throughout the first generational field, gender and class operated as powerful stabilizing influences on social relations. The reproduction of gender and class positions reinforced the solidarity of the generations. Improvements in the conditions of working-class life did take place during this period, but they did not cluster within any one particular 'lucky' birth cohort; nor was there yet the range of opportunities for leisure and consumption that could sustain the consumer segmentation of the household that characterized the second half of the twentieth century. Family, work and the resources of the locality dominated the lives of those who made up this first generational field, providing them with relatively little preparation for a life of leisure beyond the confines of these settings.

The teenage years meant work. The majority of boys and girls left school with a limited primary education and went straight into employment at the age of twelve, thirteen or fourteen. Less than 10 per cent received any formal secondary education, and less than 2 per cent a higher education.[3] In many rural areas in Europe, schooling was even more rudimentary. The impact of the media was, for the majority of the population of Europe, quite limited. As the numbers of poor people slowly declined, the poor came to occupy a marginalized position in society. For those reaching the end of their working lives, pensionerhood brought them uncomfortably close to this group of the marginalized poor.[4] Only by living with their families, in 'non-pensioner' households, did older women avoid the stigma of poverty.[5] While literacy levels improved as a consequence of universal primary education, there was little time or encouragement for extensive reading. The amount of free time available to working men and women was limited, even in the cities. The cultural practices established within one generation continued to flow through to the next, and there was little opportunity to develop a taste for leisured experience (Gallie 2000: 306, table 8.18). In short, there was no rehearsal for a future retirement lifestyle.

Retirement and pensionerhood remained the outcomes of cumulative disadvantage. Those who had not been able to acquire alternative resources ended up surviving in poor 'pensioner households'. The extent of that poverty can be gauged by the fact that, even in 1953, the average weekly expenditure of single pensioner households was less than a quarter that of the average UK household (Ministry of Labour and National Service 1957: 246–7). Fortunately, most pensioners shared a house with other, typically younger kin. Later life was still connected to, and supported by, the continuities of family and community. As Peter Townsend observed, 'the poorest people socially as well as financially were those most isolated from family life' (Townsend 1963: 34).[6]

After a life that had been dominated by work, it is not surprising that many men experienced retirement as 'a tragedy'. Townsend wrote:

> The inescapable conclusion [is] that after retirement most men in Bethnal Green could not occupy their time satisfactorily. Their life became a rather desperate search for pastimes or a gloomy contemplation of their own helplessness which . . . was little better than waiting to die. They found no substitute for the companionship, absorption and fulfilment of work. (Townsend 1963: 169)

Such experiences were confined to men. Although women did 'retire' from paid employment in the 1950s, they generally experienced work as something 'supplementary' to their life, neither central to their identity nor crucial to their sense of personal well-being. During periods of hardship – wartime, periods of unemployment, etc. – a large number of married women went out to work. Nevertheless, there was an underlying assumption, carried over from the previous century, that men should be paid a family wage sufficient to keep their wives and family at home without having to take paid work (Moehling 2001: 947–8). Consequently, women were less directly affected by 'the tragedy' of retirement. They continued to find plenty of work within the home, increasing the amount of domestic labour they performed in order to compensate for the reduced income that followed their husbands' retirement.

Women in later life, as in their earlier adult life, came to rely more upon their relations with kin than with colleagues from work. These relationships spanned the 'retirement divide' easily and uneventfully. Contacts between women of 'pensionable' age and their adult children (and some 80 per cent of women aged 60 and over in 1951 had adult children) remained frequent and intense. Nearly half had a son or daughter sharing their house, and most of those who did not saw one or other of their daughters every day. This was as true for life in the new suburbs as it was for 'traditional' working-class urban neighbourhoods (Young and Willmott 1962: 44–61; Willmott and Young 1971: 40–51). During the course of the nineteenth century, inter-generational living arrangements became more common, perhaps as a result of rising incomes (Ruggles 1987). Older people, particularly widows and widowers, continued to live in extended family households well into the twentieth century (Wall 2002). The bond between adult daughters and their ageing mothers remained strong – 'they share so much and give such help to each other because in their women's world they have the same functions of caring for home and bringing up children' (Young and Willmott 1962: 61). Gender and class, not generational differences, defined later life through-out this period.

Changes in the material culture of domestic life were slow to penetrate most European households. The process of electrifica-tion of homes that began before the First World War did not reach the majority of homes until just before the Second World War (Bowden and Offner 1996). Even then, most households did not own electrical cookers, boilers, refrigerators, or vacuum cleaners, and household maintenance depended upon manual labour – washing, scrubbing, sweeping and cooking – with the occasional use of communal facilities such as public laundries (E. Roberts 1995: 22–5). These household tasks were segregated by gender, not age. They were transmitted from one generation to the other in a manner that was largely unaffected by the intrusion of 'modern' technology (Clark and Bewley 1936). Only in middle-class households did the use of electrical household appliances such as vacuum cleaners, irons, cookers and refrigerators allow an image of the 'modern housewife' to emerge. Otherwise, through-out Europe, working-class households continued to present what one author has called 'an austere vision of modernity' (cited in Reagin 1998: 245) which did not change substantially until well after the Second World War (Davidson 1982).

Though the hours that men worked slowly fell, and paid 'family' holidays became more common, leisure, for men, was still largely confined to the local cafés, pubs or bars. For women, the demarcation between work and leisure was less clear-cut, as their lives remained tied to home and the immediate neighbourhood. While newspapers and the radio provided a widening window on the modern world, the media tended to support rather than destabilize existing social relations. With the notable exception of the cinema, the material circumstances of people's work, rest and relaxation did little to blur or challenge distinctions of class and gender; nor did they create the conditions for any divide between the generations. This was equally true for sport, the other major leisure activity that formed a key element in the mass entertainment of the early part of the twentieth century. Before and after both World Wars, attendance at football matches was predominantly a working-class activity. It reinforced the sense of localized identities and united communities, providing yet another vector for the cross-generational transmission of identity. According to John Benson, up until the late 1950s, 'young supporters tended to go to matches with their fathers and stand on the terraces with spectators of all ages' (Benson 1994: 173). The inter-generational support for local teams represented a loyalty to place that reinforced the stability of working-class lifestyles across successive cohorts born in the late nineteenth and early twentieth centuries.[7] Throughout this period, most forms of leisure served as a bridge rather than a barrier between the generations (Benson 1994: 172).

Significant change was taking place within the middle class.[8] The inter-war rise of 'professional society', to adopt Harold Perkin's phrase, provided a number of sites where 'modern' lifestyles were first actively fashioned (Perkin 1990: 242–3). Adolescence, as a distinctive phase in the lifecourse of the middle classes came to prominence at the start of the twentieth century. While most adolescents worked, and most of their wages went straight to their parents, a minority, made up of 'mostly middle class pupils in secondary education', experienced an extended period of institutionalized dependence when it was possible to rehearse a 'prototype' youth culture (Pomfret 2001). Middle-class young men and women began to form a 'post-war' generational culture, typified by the image of the 'flapper'. By the 1920s, a new cohort of economically independent young women was growing up. They were exposed to a wider variety of 'middle-class' job opportunities, a greater display of 'modern' female lifestyles, and a newly politicized sense of identity. City centre department stores, hairdressing salons, cafés and coffee shops thrived as a result 'of women going to town for a day's shopping' (Stevenson 1984: 400). Though the lifestyle of the 'bright young things' of the 1920s would shortly be eclipsed by the Depression, a cultural shift had begun amongst the younger middle classes that, with hindsight, can be seen as the precursor of the more profound generational divide that would emerge more completely after the end of the Second World War.

Meanwhile, in America . . .

The conditions that laid the foundation for the second generational field were established in the USA well before the Second World War. By 1919, America had become a truly urban society (US Census Bureau 1999), in which, for successive generations of young men and women, leisure formed an increasingly dominant motif.[9] Between 1900 and 1930, as Gary Cross has remarked, 'American prosperity gave quite ordinary citizens cars, electric gadgets, telephones and ready-to-wear fashions for which European masses would have to wait until mid-century' (Cross 2000: 17). The class conflicts that erupted in the late nineteenth and early twentieth centuries, and that continued to cause massive conflict in Europe, were marginalized by the newly confident, state-supported 'corporate culture' that established America as a consumer republic. It was a republic in which each individual was free to participate according to his or her means and ambitions (L. Cohen 2003) and in which, in the end, more chose to consume than to vote (Dumenil 1995: 53).

It was in the context of this emerging 'post-war' consumer society, that the key elements of the subsequent generational divide were fashioned. The public discourse about 'youth culture' that preoccupied US journalists, politicians and professional society in the 1920s introduced a new interpretation of modernity that privileged generation and gender over class and community as the key arenas of social and cultural change (Hirshbein 2001). First articulated in the period just before the First World War, these debates grew more extensive during the 'roaring' 1920s

(Comer 1911/1997; Bourne 1911/1997). The image, if not the reality, of the 'unity, excellence and continuity [of] American nineteenth century civilisation' was contrasted with the divisions that were opening up, throughout the modern world, of 'motors, movies, jazz-music, freedom of action, [and] liberty of thought' (Hirshbein 2001: 116, 126).

Middle-class Americans, together with a significant number of working-class people growing up in this 'modern' period spent at least some of their adolescent years as teenagers 'avant la lettre'. They had a degree of discretionary spending power, increasing opportunities to form relationships with the opposite sex, and growing exposure to the new cultural medium of the cinema, whose function was of a different order to its original role as public entertainment and show (cf. Nasow 1999). Between 1900 and 1930, US high school enrolment increased by 650 per cent, and college enrolment by 300 per cent, with the largest increase taking place in the 1920s (Fass 1979: 124). Entering the labour market during this period, members of this first post-war cohort began to swell an expanding white-collar service sector, whose aspirations were those of the 'average middle-class American' (Zunz 1998: 47–69). By the 1940s, facilitated by the growth in education and the rise of the mega-corporation during the inter-war period, these new service sector workers formed the largest occupational grouping in working America. Well before the Second World War, the majority of Americans saw themselves as 'middle class'.[10] Advertising steadily targeted this 'middle strata' of potential consumers, and in the process reframed class as 'a national ladder of consumption' (Zunz 1998: 97).

Second-generation modernity: the rise of mass culture

The generational divide that opened up in American society after the First World War was largely confined to the middle classes who possessed the discretionary spending power to participate in the new cultures of modernity. Faced with the mass hardship of the Depression and the drawing together of ranks following America's entry into the Second World War, the issue of a generational division subsided. But the idea had not been destroyed, and it soon re-emerged after the Second World War in the shape of a new social phenomenon – the American teenager. According to Thomas Hine, the term 'teenager' was introduced into the American vocabulary sometime during the Second World War. He describes the period from 1940 to 1965 as 'the classic period of the American teenager' (Hine 2000: 225). The parents of this new cohort of teenagers had themselves grown up in the inter-war years, at a time when American consumer society was establishing itself. The 'youth culture' of the 1920s had already touched their lives, and the idea of young people choosing their own wardrobe, using make-up, fashioning hairstyles, and owning motor bikes and motor cars was no longer so surprising or shocking as once it had been.[11] The post-war teenager affluence was mediated more by their parents' rising income than by any increase in teenagers' own earned income (Hine 2000: 238). Still, it was disposable income. Teenagers bought cars, radios, records and clothes, and spent time hanging out in coffee bars and drug stores, drinking, smoking and listening to music on the newly installed juke boxes that spread across America. Once the grown-ups had seated themselves comfortably in front of their television sets, the owners of commercial radio and the cinema industry soon realized that they would survive only by appealing to this new teenage audience. From this combination of post-war affluence, increasing market segmentation, and the unifying experience provided by high school culture, a generational divide was instituted that stretched across ever wider sections of American society. Cultural divisions of class and gender became less salient as Elvis Presley, James Dean and Marlon Brando presented themselves as 'rebellious' young heroes to working-class and middle-class kids alike (Cross 2000: 107). Where once they had served as an apprenticeship for lifelong labour, the teenage years became the training ground for a lifetime devoted to consumption. As this new 'youth culture' began to help shape and, in its turn, was shaped by the market, a new social rupture emerged, generating an even wider cultural divide. This was the emergence of new social movements that established a new politics around youth, freedom and identity, breaking with the previous politics of class and community that had dominated much of America's political life throughout Modernity 1.

New layers of disaffection and alienation were exposed beneath the veneer of America's affluent society, while an old division within the nation that had been kept under wraps for much of the first half of the century re-emerged with the added vengeance of youth. Race and gender moved to the forefront of American politics; and with these issues there arose new questions of identity. The 'youth culture' of the 1950s had begun to build bridges, integrating black and white, male and female, middle- and working-class cultures, helping to undermine many of the invisible because unremarked upon divisions in pre-war America (see Hine 2000: 246–8; Classen 1997). Civil rights marches took place in most US cities as summer 1964 was proclaimed 'Freedom Summer'. The mood of conflict increased, and between 1964 and 1968 American society was rocked by race riots, civil rights disturbances and anti-war protests, enacting a cultural revolution that closed down for ever the possibility of a final resolution for Modernity 1 (Piven and Cloward 1979).

After the 1973 oil crisis, many of the reforms of the 1960s slowed down or were halted. Much of the cultural revolution and its identity politics was gradually assimilated within what was now a more variegated, pervasive but passive consumer culture.[12] Real wages continued to grow, but more slowly than before, and American confidence in its consumer society began to suffer a series of temporary setbacks. The prospect of maintaining social integration through consumption had been severely challenged. Those excluded from mainstream society were excluded not so much by their inability to consume but by the fact that what they were forced to consume was an America with which they no longer wished to identify (Spigel and Curtin 1997). Subcultural styles seemed to be harbingers of new forms of social distinction, creating a vision of a more tolerant, rainbow nation. But many of these distinctions were inherently unstable. The 'counter-cultural' movements of the Sixties and early Seventies were, as Gary Cross has noted, 'premised on the revolutionary potential of youth status . . . [and] had so little to say to people farther on in life' (Cross 2000: 165). Instead, those moving further along in life developed individualized approaches toward consumption, focusing upon diffuse ideas of 'values and lifestyle'. The more solid consequences of the cultural revolution of the Sixties seemed to be the expansion of consumption, through increasing market segmentation and personal differentiation, marking a transition from 'popular' to 'mass' culture. Cross-cutting markets and segmented audiences provided the basis for an ever growing commodification of the lifeworld.

By the time of the 1980s neo-liberal reaction, lifestyle had become a dominant theme within US society, raising questions about what it is to be 'an adult' in a world where 'youthful' rebellion had become institutionalized as an unending process of individualization and continuing personal differentiation. Citizen consumers seemed to exist in infinitely divisible groupings, holding in common the desire to improve their lives, but lacking, and seeming not to desire, a shared ideal of what such improvements should look like. Earlier counter-cultural movements from the 1960s and 1970s had become 'commodified' into mainstream consumer culture. Social change in the status of women, black and Hispanic Americans, gay men and women, and other minority groups had resulted in expanding opportunities and widening life choices, but shorn of the political edge that had emerged in the 1960s. Still, these new opportunities expanded the domestic market, offering consumer choice to a widening range of citizen-participants as US poverty rates fell steadily amongst young and old, alike (Iceland 2003: 40).

If youth had acquired a new, crisis-laden identity in the Fifties and Sixties, the loss of 'youth' facing those approaching middle age in the 1980s began to move centre stage. The development of lifestyle that had emerged out of the post-war youth subcultures extended to those in mid-life who desired to hang on to the positive attributes that had been associated with their exposure to and participation in 'youth culture'.[13] For those who had grown up in this youth-privileging mass culture, for those who had been told that people over thirty had nothing to say that was worth listening to, for those who had happily listened to the young Roger Daltrey singing 'I hope I die before I get old', 'middlescence' presented a serious dilemma. The issue was as much about not losing the attributes of youth as a particular aversion to growing old. Its resolution was expressed by either denying or actively resisting ageing, or better still by doing both.[14] A new popular, self-help literature began to emerge that focused upon a youth-oriented middle age, offering reassurance to this new cohort of ageing youths that, providing certain guidelines are followed, middle age can be as exciting and challenging as youth – in fact, middle age could become a rejuvenating experience.

Central to this rejuvenation was a new approach toward health, fitness and 'activity', as more and more 'mid-lifers' donned track suits and trainers, climbed into their cars and went 'jogging', or drove down to their local 'fitness centre' for a 'work-out'. Just as marketing executives had earlier sought to capitalize on the teen market by expanding teenage lifestyles to ever younger audiences, now market researchers sought to expand market segmentation upwards by incorporating the ageing youth of the 'sixties' into the new market sector of middlesence (Luckett 1997).

Attitudes toward work were changing as significant shifts took place in attitudes toward, and expectations of, retirement. Those Americans born in the 1940s planned earlier and more deliberately for their retirement; they anticipated retiring earlier, and some were beginning to retire, at a much earlier age than those born in the earlier part of the twentieth century (Han and Moen 1999). A split was opening up between the idea of 'growing old' and the idea of 'retiring', a split reflected and fostered by the targeting in the 1980s by the American Association of Retired People of all those 'seniors' who were reaching their fiftieth birthday (Morris 1997: 41–3). The virtues of youth, of health and fitness, and the energetic pursuit of leisured lifestyles were rapidly overshadowing the virtues of work for a cohort which, socialized into consumerism as teenagers, continued to pursue their generational 'habitus' across the rest of its lifespan.

And Back in Europe . . .

In Europe, while the war babies were growing up, old age remained a poor business. Although retirement was rapidly becoming a 'normative' event, it was hardly an entrance into the leisure class. Many older people in Western Europe remained relatively poor throughout the 1950s and 1960s, and the war babies themselves hardly grew up in affluent circumstances.[15] The immediate post-war period saw little rise in earnings, and though welfare reforms were passed in many countries, their impact was slow to trickle through.[16] We have already noted the circumstances of retired people in Britain in the 1950s. Similar accounts can be found for other European countries.[17] Provisions for French pensioners immediately after the war were particularly bad, because the contributory system had not properly begun, and most retirees were forced to accept the basic minimum pension. This situation improved steadily after 1956, when an additional allowance to the basic minimum pension was introduced, and again in 1962, when the value of the minimum pension was increased. In 1971, the main pension was raised to 50 per cent of the person's notional basic salary, and workers started accumulating sufficient years of contributions to qualify for greater entitlements. Closer links between the minimum wage and the minimum pension also improved the lot of poorer pensioners (Lynes 1986). In Germany, the situation of pensioners immediately after the war was equally poor. It too began to improve after the 1957 pension reforms uprated pensions, addressing particularly the needs of rural pensioners (van Friedeberg 1958: 457–9). Broadly speaking, though, improvements in wages and salaries of working people outperformed any improvements in pension incomes during the 1950s and 1960s, leaving the retired population of Western Europe relatively worse off compared with the rising affluence of the working population.

Whilst the period between 1945 and 1954 was one of scarcity, hardship and a slow recovery of standards of living that had already been reached before the outbreak of the Second World War, the period after 1956 marked the European catch-up with the 'affluent society' across the Atlantic. What had been achieved in the USA was now dreamed about in Europe. In a West German opinion poll conducted in 1955, though only 10 per cent of households owned a fridge, over half dreamed of buying one. By 1963, fridge ownership in West Germany topped 50 per cent. Ownership of other domestic electrical appliances spread rapidly, helping to form the basis of what was perceived at the time as an enhanced 'privatism', which contrasted markedly with the public spectacles of pre-war Europe (see Abrams, Rose and Hinden 1960; Goldthorpe et al. 1968, 1969; and Zweig 1961).

As was the case in the USA, teenagers were the most evident winners in the post-war economic recovery. Their enhanced position arose from both increased earnings and increased allowances; but in Europe, teenagers received more of their income from earnings than they did from parental allowances, since fewer stayed on at high school compared with American teenagers in the 1950s. The collective socialization of Europe's teenagers into a common 'youth culture' was consequently less comprehensive than in the USA. Still, by the 1960s the dominance of class over culture was beginning to break down within the lives of Europe's teenagers. The ending of rationing, the post-war housing boom and rising household incomes saw an increased exposure to contemporary American culture, a culture which had already come to symbolize plenty, as America had survived the Second World War to become undoubtedly the world's greatest economic power. America's musical tastes, its food and drink, TV and films, fashion and style, accentuated 'youth' as the new site of social distinction and cultural change. Many of the problems that American popular music faced at home, like the white middle-class anxiety over class and issues of racial integration (Hine 2000: 240–8) were scarcely relevant to the new European teenage market. For Europe's teenagers, American youth culture represented colour, excitement, sexuality, freedom and fun (Akhtar and Humphries 2001).

In the context of a general increase in affluence that affected nearly all age-groups in the 1950s and 1960s, the creation of a new generational field depended upon the agency of youth. For a variety of reasons, teenagers were best placed to benefit from the new post-war surplus. They were freer to spend, and there was more and more for them to spend their money on. Such disposable income fostered greater inter-generational social differentiation. There were new opportunities to develop youth 'subcultures' based upon dress, music, sex and style, that were exercised in places set apart from the sites of traditional middle- or working-class culture.[18] What formed a common theme within this process of social differentiation was the privileging of youth as the dominant cultural force of the times, which challenged the values of both middle-class and working-class patriarchs alike.

By the 1960s youth and youthfulness were valorized throughout Europe. If the inter-war years had been a time when class-based revolutions seemed imminent, the 1960s were a time when a generational revolution appeared to be in the offing. As Pierre Bourdieu (1992) has pointed out, cultural consumption has always been predisposed, consciously and deliberately, to fulfil a social function of legitimating social differences. The changes in cultural consumption in the 1960s were presaged upon a change in focus for such social distinctions. Generational rather than class- or gender-based differences were more salient, differences that were much more explicitly cultural in their origins and expression. The 'revolution' on the streets, in the clubs and coffee bars, in the dance halls and on the college campuses, was a revolt as much against the style of the older generation as against the oppression of classes or nations. It was a disdain and a dislike directed against all those who had maintained and managed Modernity 1, and not only its ruling elites. The cultural divide that members of this second post-war cohort were fashioning was intended quite deliberately to exclude a whole generation.

In Germany, the after-effects of the Nazi regime added greater depth and complexity to this divide. Family life had undergone 'a process of swift and radical modernization in the early 1950s . . . making family law more democratic and individualistic' than elsewhere in Europe (Schultheis 1997: 59). Within this newly individualistic family setting, the younger generation wanted to know nothing about their National Socialist past. Given this ambivalence and the extensive penetration of American power and culture during the post-war reconstruction, German youth were among the vanguard in welcoming the new transatlantic music, fashions and lifestyle. The division of the country and the differences in material lifestyle between East and West added weight to the value attached to this new 'democratic' consumer culture, while providing a readier framing of the generational divide between the values of the 'young' West Germany and the rejection of the culture and values of the older, deeply compromised generation. It is no coincidence, then, that the Beatles' international career as musical and cultural icons was launched not in London or Liverpool but in Hamburg.

The transmission of American consumer culture created more conflict in post-war France than in the rest of Europe. Although France's post-war economic development more than matched that of Britain, with rises in income, living standards and expanding access to durable goods such as TV, radio, cars and refrigerators, there was a more determined national resistance to the 'contamination' of French culture by American cultural imports. Quotas were maintained on Hollywood films; there was resistance to playing rock-and-roll music on French radio, and active opposition to the dubbing and broadcasting of American TV programmes. Nevertheless, the state-mediated protection of French culture failed to isolate French youth, who brought a greater degree of political passion and imagination to the social and cultural 'youth' movements of the 1960s than elsewhere in Europe. Protests against American militarism and its consumer imperialism were integrated with protests about the 'reactionary elitism' and oppressive sexual codes of the country's class-dominated educational system. The tripling of student numbers from the 1930s to the 1960s added weight to the students' voice. But any demonstrations of class unity between workers and students ran foul of the new generational divide that was opening up on the Left. Unsurprising, then, that workers and students formed an uneasy alliance in 1968, when the Communist CGT first denounced, then later supported, the students before becoming distracted by the forthcoming general election, which the student radicals denounced as a bourgeois fraud. In the end, the combined class and generational divides between the middle-aged working-class leadership of the CGT and middle-class radical youth proved too wide to span a political revolution.

What the events of spring 1968 represented was a growing desire to bring to an end the old order and to build a world that would be freer from the constraints and limitations of the past. That youth should be at the vanguard of this new social movement is not surprising, but that youth became its central focus was. What was condemned was a generation as much as a class. The clamour for personal freedoms (for example, the protests over restricted access to single-sex student accommodation) mixed with calls for an end of class exploitation (for example, the call for a general strike) characterized much of the Sixties political turmoil. Students treated the posters of foreign revolutionary heroes like Che Guevara and Ho Chi Minh as equivalent to Sixties' pop stars, film stars and other cultural celebrities. The Sixties represent a unique cultural watershed whose boundaries were formed by a generational divide that has successfully spanned classes, communities and continents. It has made the third age a phenomenon of increasing global significance.

Ageing Societies and the Post-Generational Divide

During the decades that have followed the Sixties, it is possible to discern a common cultural social and economic pathway that members of this 'post-generational' cohort have followed. Its origins lie in the cultural and economic transformations that took place in the Sixties and Seventies, but the course that this post-generational lifestyle has followed has been modified continuously by changing generational habitus. The contexts for many of these changes are presented in summary form in table 5.1.

The young men who started work after the First World War were following in the footsteps of their fathers. Like their fathers, they were city dwellers with relatively little education, occupying rented accommodation and possessing little in the way of significant household amenities. They lived in highly gendered communities bound by ties of kinship, and followed a pattern of life that was dominated by paid and unpaid work. Although the world around them was undergoing rapid technological and social transformation, for the majority, these changes remained, if not invisible, certainly out of reach. Ensuring that there was enough food on the table, clothes on their backs, and support and contact with kin remained the central concern for most families both before and after the First World War (Clark and Bewley 1936). In the decade after the end of the Second World War, when this cohort was beginning to retire from the work-force, their economic well-being rested primarily upon a combination of family support and the state pension. Throughout the 1950s and 1960s there were gradual improvements in the replacement value of old age pensions and old age social security payments, reflecting national concerns to manage the growing vulnerability of a pensioner population that was becoming more dependent upon the state for its support.

The young men and women who started work in the 1960s grew up in a world where technological changes had become commonplace. There were more new houses, better-paid jobs and more 'labour-saving' technology within the home. Even if the work places of the 1960s were still the mines, docks, railways, shops and factories of the pre-war industrial era, working conditions were improving, and labour was more able to command national respect. Faced with the mass culture of national TV and radio networks, the popular culture of the neighbourhood declined. People were gradually socialized into styles of consumption that enabled people of all ages to participate in a mass culture designed to satisfy personal needs and individual desires.

If the middle-aged dominated the culture of Modernity 1, youth led the movement into Modernity 2. Clothing, music, personal care and entertainment were the areas where the greatest expansion of consumption occurred, and the fastest-growing consumer market was that made up by newly affluent young people. As this second post-war generation begin preparing to retire, they can look back over a lifetime of cumulative advantage. Rising affluence has ensured that consumption has grown in importance. By the end of the twentieth century, leisure goods and services have become the major source of household expenditure for people of all ages. Home has become a central site for consumption, while the surrounding neighbourhood has declined in its social and cultural significance. The ability to maintain social connectedness no longer depends upon physical proximity with the exception of those most intimate of tasks that are normally performed by the individual him- or herself, or if not by those sharing one's bed and one's bathroom. The majority of households have access to both a car and a telephone, and most householders now have a mobile (cell) phone as well. Direct social contacts between neighbours have become less common than in the past, but living alone no longer bears the stigma that it once did. More and more households are formed by one person alone, a phenomenon that reflects choice as often as necessity.

Private and public spheres intersect in the 'everyday experience' that forms part of the mass culture. Thanks to the

Table 5.1 The generational divide between Modernity 1 and Modernity 2

	Modernity 1, 1880s to 1950s	Modernity 2, 1960s –
Cultural	A homogenous 'popular culture' existing side by side with an equally homogenous 'high culture'.	Consumer culture incorporates popular and high culture into a cross-cutting, inclusive, individualized and highly segmented mass culture.
	Styles of life are powerfully segmented by class and gender.	Age segregation operates more powerfully than either gender or class segmentation.
	Inter-generational cultural continuities are maintained by the interconnections of kinship and community.	The great generational divide of the Sixties destabilizes and blurs subsequent cohort distinctions.
	Work – whether at home or in the workplace – dominates styles of living.	Consumption is at the centre of lifestyles and social identities.
Economic	Dominance of industrial capitalism.	Dominance of financial capitalism.
	Close connection between the control and ownership of capital.	Disconnection between the control and ownership of capital.
	Main division between a wage-earning working class and a salary-earning middle class.	Increased part-time and own account working.
	Dominance of patriarchy and the family wage.	Decline of collective pay and rewards systems.
	Reducing economic inequalities within classes.	Growing individual inequalities alongside declining structural inequalities (around gender, class and ethnicity).

Political	High level of polarization between 'pro-business' and 'pro-labour' political parties. The nation as the focus of a common identity. Growing role of the state as the necessary broker in the social compact between labour and capital. The 'bureaucratic individualization' of the lifecourse.	Decline in political participation and demise of class-based party allegiances. Dominance of issue and identity politics. Retrenchment of the state as an administrative structure regulating the 'conduct of conduct'. Shift towards an individualized reliance upon market solutions (re-commodification and de-institutionalization of the lifecourse).
Social	The dominance of the community as the site of social life. Parents the key figures in the reproduction of everyday life. The insecurity of the many sustaining the security of the few. Consumption dominated by the immediate needs for food and shelter. Work, home and leisure as collectively gendered worlds. (Male) retirement as the collapse of the autonomous social agent.	The demise of communities of propinquity. Dominance of peer groups and partners over parents and parenting. The insecurities of all in conditions of mass security. Necessary consumption becomes subordinate to the consumption of identity and community. Work, home and leisure increasingly individualized experiences. Retirement as the continuation of individualized consumption-oriented lifestyles.

proliferation of satellite, cable and 'terrestrial' television channels and the growing scope of the Internet, people can exchange endless versions of 'everyday life'. This greater transparency in the lives that people lead fosters a greater reflexivity in the styling of life. The cultural revolution of the Sixties has evolved into a 'permanent revolution', transforming the meaning and social identities of youth, adulthood and later life. Since the 1930s, successive birth cohorts have been incorporated into the post-war lifestyle of what we have learned to call the Sixties' generation, members of which have continued to develop, expand and extend the mass culture that the young people of the Fifties and Sixties helped to introduce.

This new generational field is no longer confined to, nor defined by, any particular cohort or generational unit. It no longer depends upon a particular habitus being formed in adolescence which then colonizes the rest of life. As the field itself expands, it creates new challenges which demand new responses and which provide new habitus at different points along the lifecourse. Health is a case in point, and private pensions another. The emphasis on fitness and self-promoting health that emerged in the late Seventies has transformed running and swimming from activities associated with high school and college to ones that permeate the lives of grown-ups at all ages. Likewise, it has fostered a widening range of 'leisure wear', 'cosmaceuticals' and 'nutraceuticals', personal weight training equipment, bicycle and rowing machines, and an expanding membership of private gyms and 'leisure centres'.

Personal finances and private investments are equally products of this post-war era. Following the collapse of the Bretton Woods agreement and the rise of neo-liberalism in the 1980s, pensions and investments have started to become matters of common interest and common concern to more and more young and late middle-aged people. Personal finance sections began appearing in both the 'quality' and the 'popular' press shortly after the sale to the general public of shares in public utilities and nationalized industries. Since then there has been a growing emphasis upon personal investments and personal pension plans, stimulated in Britain by the privatization of the State Earnings Related Pension in the early 1980s. This growing emphasis upon self-reliance has begun to shape a new 'economic habitus' for larger numbers of middle-aged people (Peggs 2000). Personal fitness and individual financial viability have become lifestyle commodities demanded by adults of all ages. The youth of the 1960s were not striving to look young or become rich; they wanted primarily to express their distance from the old by making themselves appear more flamboyantly radical. But as the youth of that period have grown older, they have sought to retain the value and status of that 'youth culture'. They continue to care about clothing, about fashion, and about appearance, and they continue to care about having the freedom to spend. By equating health with looking good, and by treating fitness and the capacity to consume as moral imperatives (see Lupton 1995), they have enabled 'generational markets' eager to package and sell these qualities to emerge. The audience for these new products is no longer confined to a particular cohort or a particular age-group. Hair dyes, anti-wrinkling creams, 'fight the flab' diets, vitamin and mineral supplements, sportswear and gym membership, have an appeal that extends across ever widening birth cohorts, making 'anti-ageing' an integral part of mass culture.

It is this division – a division periodized in various ways as the transition from popular to mass culture, from organized to disorganized capitalism, from Modernity 1 to Modernity 2 – that marks out the cultural boundaries of the third age. Central to this transformation has been the progressive socialization of personal consumption. As more and more of the lifeworld has been successfully incorporated into the system world of the market, the state has ceased to exercise its original role in securing and 'institutionalizing' the lifecourse. Those born at the turn of the nineteenth century saw their social and civic identities made integral to the nation by the expansion of the institutions of the state. The stability that the state was able to achieve during the lifecourse of members of that first-generation modernity has long since failed to meet the aspirations that it first engendered. The market has proved quicker to spot those aspirations, and keener to support and extend them. The state was not designed to compete with the market in sustaining and expanding mass culture, which has now overshadowed the 'older' culture of need that the state successfully displaced. The transition from state to corporate solutions that emerged in the USA in the aftermath of the First World War has been replayed, some fifty years later, in Western Europe. The post-Second World War solution of the welfare state has begun seriously to founder in the complications of the fiscal crisis of the state, but instead of a widely anticipated 'legitimation crisis' (Habermas 1988; O'Connor 1987), what has occurred is a re-commodification of later life.

The retirement experiences of US senior citizens in the 1950s are now being replayed in an anxious social Europe. Back then, US retirees were hailed as 'today's leisure class' (Michelon 1954: 371). Although people enjoying an amenity-rich retirement were at the time a very small minority of the US retired population, their reality formed the retirement aspirations of a growing majority. Now participation in mass culture characterizes all but a small minority. Market segmentation cross-cuts the lifecourse, destabilizing the former certainties of class, generation and gender. Identities that are dependent upon consumption are more difficult to manage than those which are contingent upon labour force participation. Lifestyles supported through consumption are less easily assimilated into models of citizenship, and the risks of lifestyle failure are not so easily managed by the state. Inevitably, there is a shift towards personal responsibility. A 'youth culture' can afford to act irresponsibly, happily dismissing the limitations of a past it feels unconnected to, and readily inflating the possibilities of a future it imagines as its own. But having accumulated a history of permanent consumption over most of their lifecourse, the dilemma facing the ageing participants of post-war youth culture is whether their mass retirement will still enable them to celebrate an ever-expanding mass culture. The advent of an ageing society will seriously test the future of such post-generational lifestyles.

6

Community and the Nature of Belonging

If the study of cohorts and generations emphasizes historical contingency in the social and cultural ordering of the lifecourse, the study of communities, by contrast, emphasizes the 'grounding' of the life cycle within the constancies of place and person. Whereas cohorts qualify and particularize identity, community roots it. While class and generation are defined through conflict and change, community represents stability and security. The privatism of domestic relationships is contrasted with the public altruism of communal relationships. Impersonal, state-mediated institutional care is set against the personal care offered by members of the community. The distrust and individualization of modern life are compared unfavourably with the solidarity and shared values of 'traditional' communities. Within community, individual identities are acknowledged, understood and valued; in the wider society they are ignored.

Community has always served as a normative point of reference in the social sciences (Nisbet 1970. 21, Bauman 2001: 1). The strongly moralized values attached to the term have made it difficult dispassionately to research 'community', and despite a considerable body of research, little progress seems to have been made in constructing 'a theory of community'. That at least was the conclusion reached by Bell and Newby in their review of community studies in the 1970s. Instead of continuing to treat 'community' as an 'object' of study, they proposed that 'community studies' should be considered primarily as a methodological approach to the study of households, families and class relations (Bell and Newby 1971: 54–81). Others suggested abandoning the concept altogether (Macfarlane 1977). Although such positions still have their advocates, subsequent developments suggest that their conclusions were premature.

The cultural turn in the social sciences drew attention to identity as a central feature of contemporary life. 'Community' acquired a new significance as the symbolic arena in which individual social identities are created, expressed and supported. Linked with this cultural approach has been the growing politicization of 'community' both in a symbolic sense, as in 'communities of identity', and in a topographical sense, as in 'local community politics'. The cultural revolution of the 1960s shifted the focus of social conflict away from class interests to communal identities. The 'new' politics that emerged sought equal recognition of cultural 'minorities' and the promotion of their social and civic rights (Fraser 1995). Claims for a more equal distribution of the nation's social and cultural capital acquired greater urgency as demands for greater redistribution of its material surplus seemed on the point of being realized. The demand for recognition of the neglected social and cultural spaces of minorities were themselves followed by a renewed concern regarding the plight of economically marginalized 'neighbourhoods' left behind as the new residuum of post-industrial society. The spread of affluence in the decades following the end of the Second World War created the conditions for a politics of the personal. This highlighted the cultural and political exclusion of minorities. The restructuring of the economy in the 1980s created new forms of highly localized, welfare-dependent social, cultural and economic impoverishment. Poverty in post-scarcity society was no longer framed as a site of struggle between wage labour and the property-owning classes. Rather, the concern of the Eighties was the existence of an 'underclass' emerging in the aftermath of the lurch toward a 'post-industrial' society. The idea of the underclass as a spatially concentrated and socially excluded group drew attention as much to the *housing* as to the *employment* circumstances of the individuals assigned to this category. While the concerns over marginalized identities were first articulated by nationally active bodies which quickly expanded to become globalized social movements, the focus upon marginalized *localities* arose as pockets of social disorder spilled out beyond their social or geographical confines, threatening the coherence of the post-war social compact.

If the dominant response of the state to movements based upon communities of identity has been to engage actively with and incorporate their agendas both locally, nationally and inter-governmentally, the response to neighbourhood communities has been more muted. Most government strategies for such 'unwelcome' problems have been to invest 'ring-fenced' moral and material capital into these 'unruly' neighbourhoods through a combination of 'regeneration' programmes and improved security (see Wallace 2001; Giddens 2000: 48–9; Tam 1998: 120–9; Putnam 2001: 317–18). While the politics of community extends equally to communities of identity and 'neighbourhood' communities, it does so in very different ways and with very different results.

Structural and post-structural approaches share a focus upon community as a site of cultural meaning and a source of belonging within the wider social world. Where they differ is in whether communities are defined primarily by their structural-material or by their symbolic-cultural boundaries. As the organization of the 'social product' and its consumption has changed, communities based upon 'propinquity' have grown less significant. The means by which individuals gain their income and spend their money depend less and less upon spatially bound institutions. No longer do towns, villages and neighbourhoods grow up around single industries; nor is household consumption dependent upon local shops or neighbourhood stores. Whether this reflects the 'eclipse' of community or merely a shift in the way that community is defined is a central element in this debate. Some, like Anthony Cohen, have argued that, 'whether or not its structural boundaries remain intact . . . people construct community symbolically making it a resource and repository of meaning and a referent of their identity' (A. P. Cohen 1989: 118). From this perspective, changes in the social and economic organization of society lead not to the demise of community but to transformation in the way it is represented. If those landmarks that once defined 'neighbourhood' prove incapable of sustaining its communal identity, other markers will emerge serving a similar symbolic function.

Critics of such an avowedly culturalist approach argue that communities are more than repositories of meaning. They represent material, social and emotional ties, which can only be constructed and maintained through regular, face-to-face interaction (Calhoun 1998). The experience of being part of a supportive social network, they argue, is more important in sustaining an individual's sense of belonging than the ephemeral ties of an identity based upon a particular set of shared interests. Only by having access to more generalized support – i.e. support that is not contingent upon sharing a particular identity – can people be considered to be living within a community. From such a perspective, the study of community becomes the study of social life as 'communal life'. Rather than treating 'community' as a geographical or cultural space, community becomes a variable, the quality of social relations – 'the way in which specific social actors are linked to each other' (Calhoun 1980: 116). In place of community, we are left with its residue – 'community-ness'.

In the rest of this chapter we shall explore in more detail the evolution of the concept of community within the social sciences. In doing so, we aim to show that these conceptual shifts are themselves reflective of historical change in the nature and organization of social relations. Despite changes in both the location and representation of community, and the direct and unmediated linkage between the individual and both the state and the market, there exists a need for structures that moderate the effects of such 'individualization'. The original formulation of this dilemma – between the need for the constancies and support of a community and the desire for social change and personal improvement – remains the work of Frederick Tönnies (1958), and it is to his work we first turn.

Frederick Tönnies and the Demise of 'Traditional' Society

Frederick Tönnies' classic account, *Gemeinschaft und Gesellschaft* ('Community and Association', 1958) provides a logical starting point to address the 'problem of community', just as Mannheim's work offers a *fons et origo* for any discussion of the nature of 'cohorts' and 'generations'. When Tönnies first published his account, the industrialization of Western Europe was well under way, and the economic system was already moving toward a form of 'impersonal capitalism' (Savage and Miles 1994: 48). The process of class formation that had its origins in the late eighteenth and early nineteenth centuries was pretty much complete. The villages left behind by the urban migrants were the dwelling places of a dying culture, which was viewed with a distinctly romantic nostalgia. Cities were where the new modernity was manufactured; they were the key sites of social conflict and social change. The pace of life and work and the insecurities of both created a sense of excitement as well as a widespread unease amongst the literate classes. There was a desire to re-establish some solidity and security, and for many, the rural community filled that role. Slow-moving, conservative and closer to nature, the countryside provided a point of contrast, a moral economy that represented a cloak of comfort to those experiencing the chill winds of change.

For Tönnies, the population movement from villages to towns and cities represented an inexorable shift in social relations, which he described as a move from community (*Gemeinschaft*) to society (*Gesellschaft*). Community represented a unitary whole, a 'one-class' society (Laslett 1983); by contrast, society was a formalized and somewhat fragmented network of associations created through explicit, rational principles. These principles, as Tönnies saw it, derived from a particular bourgeois rationality, designed not that men in general might prosper, but that a particular class might do so. As political conflict and technological change increased, and as communication became more complex and sophisticated, the urban environment became less stable and less secure. Faced with the divisions of class society, Tönnies argued, a new urban *burgerliche gesellschaft* (bourgeois society) was being created which sought to impose a degree of social 'unity' comparable to that which had characterized rural *volksgemeinschaft* (folk community). The means of achieving this new form of solidarity were the growing administrative organs of the nation-state (Tönnies 1958: 27–9). For Tönnies, anticipating both Gramsci (1957) and Althusser (1969, 1971), the state was now charged with the task of making society function as a community – but for the principle benefit of one particular section of that society, the urban bourgeoisie.

No doubt the rural community that the nineteenth-century city immigrants had left behind never possessed quite such harmony or such unity of purpose as was later credited to it. Certainly it had not been able to ensure the lifelong moral and material security of all. Disease, famine, wars, disputes, deceits and other more personal disasters left many in a state of rural impoverishment that could never be allayed by the institutions of rural society – whether of the village or of the market town. But the underlying principles of the *ancien regime* did purport to offer a common framework to make sense of the distress, disease and disadvantage of rural life. It was a unifying framework, after all, and one that stood in contrast to the evident divisions of the new urban society. It also served as a constant point of reference that could be invoked both by reactionary writers who sought to lambaste all forms of modern social development as well as by more radical reformers who wanted to establish a form of socialism based on such communal principles.

Against this background of urbanization, social conflict and the emergence of class-segregated neighbourhoods, it is understandable that those who first sought to formalize the study of this new society should seek to define it by contrasting it with its seeming antithesis. Life in the village was contrasted with life in the city; in the village relations were characterized by their 'closeness', in the city by their 'distance'; village society was distinguished by its sense of 'unity', urban society by its 'conflicts'; village life was 'stable' and 'predictable', city life was filled with 'uncertainty' and 'change'. This dichotomy formalized by Tönnies as the distinction between 'community' and 'society' has remained a central feature of the social sciences. The modern nation-state is seen to have arisen out of the destruction of the old regime's 'traditional society'. Judgements of whether this was a good or a bad 'thing' have varied, and even the classical writers seem to have vacillated in reaching a conclusion. But what Tönnies and other nineteenth-century writers failed to acknowledge was that within the new towns and cities of industrial society, new forms of communities were already appearing. Eventually their 'traditions' of support and self-help would serve as another reference point for later generations of social scientists, who would, in their turn, lament the passing of these solid 'traditional' working-class communities (Redfield 1955; Stein 1964).

Neighbourhoods and Urban Sociology

What was different about the new urban society was the plurality of cultural and social interests it contained. Communities unified on the basis of class (neighbourhoods) existed within a wider community that was profoundly divided by class (the city). As the working classes became a recognized political force and were gradually incorporated as partners in the civic enterprise of twentieth-century society, the problems of social integration that had been so evident in the nineteenth-century grew a little less critical. In the context of developments in city planning and urban management (Wilcox 1904; Munroe 1926), a new interest emerged in the city as a site of social order, and not just disorder. This was exemplified by the work of Robert Park and members of the so-called Chicago School (Park 1952).

The new urban sociology focused attention upon the 'neighbourhood', geographically and often ethnically distinct urban communities that constituted sites of active social life, supportive of both family integrity as well as individual development. While Park recognized that cities could be sites of potential conflict, deviance and danger, he valued the city as 'the natural habitat of civilized man'.[1] For the new urban sociologists, the city represented a progressive environment in which numerous communities could coexist, each capable of providing its own form of moral order within the broader society. This enthusiastic modernism offered a counterbalance to the nostalgia for a lost community that Tönnies and other European sociologists had fostered. Although the enthusiasms of urban sociology would wane, in the early decades of the twentieth century, the Chicago School represented a positive affirmation of the social worth of cities and the capacity of individuals to re-create a set of values and a sense of belonging wherever they found themselves.

Throughout the first half of the twentieth century, urban life dominated Western societies. Life in the local neighbourhood was interconnected by kinship and integrated across the generations. It was also highly gendered. Men would leave for work by bicycle, bus, tram, train or on foot to join a segregated 'occupational community', returning in the evenings to eat and maybe drink in the local bars, pubs or cafés with other men who shared similar experiences of work, home and locality. The women stayed behind, spending their days within the neighbourhood, carrying out domestic chores, visiting the local shops, and looking after the children before and after they went to school. In the absence of such home amenities as washing machines, fridges, central heating, indoor bathrooms, electric cookers and vacuum cleaners, household chores necessitated frequent incursions into public spaces. There was a need to make daily visits to the local shops and markets, or to take washing to the local laundries. Wet clothes had to be hung out to dry in the streets and on the balconies. The local neighbourhood was interspersed with kinship networks, and social life naturally extended to the streets and alleyways, shops and halls, that constituted the common space where most of the urban working class lived. For entertainment there were the local pubs, cafés, beer halls and bars, and, increasingly, the local cinema. Cities were where people lived, and neighbourhoods were the predominant settings in which communal life took place. As Murray Bookchin writes:

> [T]hroughout much of the nineteenth and early twentieth centuries, displacement was followed by resettlement and recommunalisation, even in the most desperately poor slums of the overpopulated cities of Europe and America. The pub in the industrial cities of England, the café in France, and the beer hall in Germany, no less than the various community centers, around which the ethnic ghettos formed in New York and other American cities, provided foci for a distinctly working class culture, largely artisan in its outlook, class-oriented in its politics and knitted together by mutual self-help groups. (Bookchin 1997: 189)

Within these urban neighbourhoods, the strongest bond that tied people to each other, that conferred a sense of belonging, was still that of kinship. To quote John Benson: 'the community consciousness of the poor derived essentially from the twin pillars of kinship and neighbourhood ... [and] it was in the streets that members of the community came together to talk and play, to work and shop and to observe ... the incursions of intruders' (Benson 1989: 132).

The demise of the urban neighbourhood began in the inter-war period with the rise of middle-class suburbs; but the real change came in the wake of the Second World War. Across Europe a massive programme of rebuilding and re-housing took place. Instead of repairing or restoring the old city neighbourhoods, the opportunity was taken to build new estates, using new materials, with improved standards of heating, lighting and plumbing, where each flat or house was furnished with a range of domestic facilities that previously would have been found only in middle-class houses. This massive programme of re-housing led to a resurgence of interest in 'community studies', as government-backed social scientists sought to establish the strengths and weaknesses of the old and the new 'communities'.

Young and Willmott's *Family and Kinship in East London*, first published in 1957, reflects this mix of nostalgia for the old and optimism for the new. Writing about the post-war need for urban regeneration, they argued:

> people will have to move within their own district if not outside it as the slums beyond salvage are cleared and replaced. . . . [The authorities'] negative task is to demolish slums . . . their positive one to build new houses and new towns cleaner and more spacious than the old. Yet even when the town planners have set themselves to create communities anew as well as houses they have still put their faith in buildings sometimes speaking as though all that was necessary . . . for community spirit [was] a community centre. (Young and Willmott 1962: 198)

But within the wider, national community, a change was evident in the mood and manners of the times. If the years immediately after the Second World War were characterized by continuing hardship sustained by feelings of moral worth and national solidarity, once the economic recovery began gathering speed during the 1950s, a new mood of impatience with the old ways began to appear. People wanted to see real changes in their own lives. France was poised for its *trentes glorieuses*; Germany – or at least West Germany – was about to set off on its path toward *Wirtschaftswunder*; while Italy, liberated from its own past demons, was beginning to entertain the idea of the *dolce vita*. Britain would simply be told that it had 'never had it so good'.

Mass consumer society had begun to arrive from across the Atlantic, and with it came the promise of increased social mobility and ever improving lives. After the 1960s cultural revolution and the associated political movements of Marxism and feminism, community studies seemed all but dead.[2]

We have discussed the generational fault line that emerged during the Sixties in the preceding two chapters. The massive rehousing programme that took place during this period led to millions of people finding themselves in new houses, with new lives, surrounded by new household facilities. Bathrooms and indoor toilets, fridges and washing machines, TVs and telephones, became standard features of 1960s household.[3] As the home became a richer and more resourceful place, the locality – the neighbourhood – became less significant in meeting people's needs for support, assistance and identity. A palpable improvement took place in the material circumstances of most people's lives, shifting attention away from the local community toward the wider social world. In the process, a significant cultural exchange was enacted. The warmth and solidarity of the 'old' neighbourhood was replaced by the warmth and solidarity of the 'new' home. As Europe's economies grew, the post-war welfare state expanded, extending its guarantees of support in times of need. The economic optimism generated by full employment and rising incomes was reflected in a growing desire amongst younger members of the working-class population to leave their old neighbourhoods and make their way up in the world. This shift was observed in opinion polls and reflected in novels, plays and films of the time. The British 'New Wave' exemplified this process, when a series of novels turned into films reiterated the restlessness and dissatisfaction of the 'new' working class. Typical of this genre were *Room at the Top, Saturday Night and Sunday Morning, Loneliness of the Long Distance Runner, A Taste of Honey, A Kind of Loving, Billy Liar, This Sporting Life*, etc. (see Marwick 1998: 118–43). Community was something to be left behind: it was a drag, fit only for those too old or too set in their ways to move on (cf. Bourke 1994: 158–9). Young people on the brink of 'adulthood' were not interested in community, new or old; they wanted instead to establish a separate identity for themselves – an identity marked more by its style than by its solidarities (cf. Hebdige 1979).[4]

The Rise of Symbolic Community

Allied to this new preoccupation with personal freedom and the expression of 'identity' was the new academic discipline of 'Cultural Studies'. Cultural Studies was as much a product of the Sixties as pop art, pop music and popular television. Questions of lifestyle and identity were its central themes, and they were central concerns for many young people in the 1960s. This was a cohort on the move, made more conscious through the expanding media that 'the times they are a' changing'. Older generations were in danger of being left behind. Working class was becoming not just a position within the system of production, but a culturally 'trendy' identity, representing a new kind of cultural capital within the world of popular entertainment. Photographers, artists, novelists, TV directors, musicians, designers all happily lined themselves up as 'working class'. This new cultural identity for the working class led to a plethora of writing about the embourgeoisement of the working classes, the culture of the affluent worker, and so on. But although unionization and working-class activism continued, the political centre of gravity was already moving. A distance had been created between sign and signifier, and the majority of the working class were leaving behind their attachments to the old occupational communities, the shared communal hardships, and the inter-generational solidarities of the past.

For those enjoying neither the benefits of youth nor the consolations of old age, the unifying focus was the home and home building. This was reinforced by the growing influence of TV. In 1962, according to one British survey, people spent about one-third of their leisure time watching TV, more time than was spent on any other single activity apart from work and sleeping, leading one commentator to argue that 'the amount of time spent viewing television and the narrow cultural choice available suggest that television seems to be imposing a cultural classlessness . . . which would never have been considered possible or desirable in the past' (Millar 1966: 233). TV acted as an intermediary between the private world of home, the household economy, and the wider public world – the national community. In Europe, TV was dominated initially by state broadcasting companies that delivered a carefully regulated diet of programmes designed to inform, entertain and engage the whole population. Although TV was capable of reflecting and reproducing class, gender and generational divides, it did so through a medium that was essentially genderless, classless and trans-generational, delivering the same messages in the same way to each household within its broadcasting range. From the Fifties through to the Seventies, the number of channels available to TV viewers, outside the United States, was extremely limited. Multi-channel surfing and the market segmentation that accompanied it was simply not possible. Even if the neighbourhood had diminished as a site of social interaction, something of the 'symbolic' nature of community and neighbourhood life was still capable of being represented through the agency of national, domestic TV programming.

The dominant role of the mass media, the expansion of telecommunication systems, the interconnectedness of national societies, and the 'neophiliac' desire to leave the past and its old-fashioned communities behind formed key elements in the 1960s' cultural revolution. This cultural shift led Melvin Webber to argue that within a more middle-class society people 'no longer [belong to a] community of place . . . but [to] an interest community which within a freely communicating society need not be spatially concentrated [since] we are increasingly able to interact with each other wherever we may be located' (Webber 1963: 29). Although Webber's perspective has been criticized, he was one of the first writers, alongside Marshall McLuhan, to acknowledge the transformation in social relationships taking place in the Sixties. This transformation can be understood as the loss (once again) of community as 'neighbourhood' and its rebirth as a virtual space within an emerging mass culture in which social relationships are no longer dominated by the structures of 'propinquity'.

From 1960 onwards, millions of British households found themselves regularly drawn to the TV to watch the weekly goings-on of a virtual community, *Coronation Street*, the first and longest-running soap opera on British TV (Little 2000). Based upon life in a notionally working-class street in a northern English town, the 'soap' was devised by a young gay writer, Tony Warren. Warren's own career mirrored the British New Wave, he moved from a background steeped in working-class traditions to become a major player in the media industry. *Coronation Street* was an immediate hit, whose appeal extended across all social classes and engaged all generations. From the very first episode, older people formed some of the central characters in the series. The longer the programme's run, the more they became constant points of reference, serving as 'the elders' of this post-war ersatz community. Gradually the older generation were written out of the script or died, and *Coronation Street* became dominated by younger characters addressing more controversial social issues of wider relevance than those of the neighbourhood. The 'street' has become a free-floating signifier, its introductory shot (a view of wet slate roofs and the backs of a small row of working-class terraced houses) as much a trademark of the series as a visual representation of its points of origin. Reflecting, far more than creating, the changing times in which it has been broadcast, the characters who first appeared in the series as 'old people' were nominally in their early or mid-sixties. Younger characters who have since reached similar ages to those of the original cast of 'old people' still remain frozen in a kind of middle age, entering and exchanging or refusing relationships much as they always have. When the series began in the 1960s, the most frequently appearing characters included Albert Tatlock (a widower in his mid-sixties), Jack and Annie Walker (a married couple in their early sixties), Minnie Caldwell and Ena Sharples (two widows in their early sixties). These characters were played as feisty 'pensioners'. Forty years on, the central characters who have still 'survived' from the 1960s include the long-lived Ken Barlow (now in his early sixties and still playing the same 'Lothario' role) and 'the eternal spinster', Emily Bishop (now in her early seventies). Age no longer roots this particular virtual community.

Soap operas provide a core element of TV programming around the world, and one of the core functions they seem to perform is to sustain the idea of 'community':

> almost without exception the macro-narratives of all the major soaps and telenovelas in most of the countries analysed . . . promote the values of solidarity, caring for and about others, defending other people's rights, compromise and cooperation. . . .

They create communities based on solidarity and sharing, but also communities which are open, participatory and democratic. (O'Donnell 1998: 227–8)

Their influence depends upon the assumed power of the mass media to re-create a set of rules for social relationships that have traditionally been seen as 'communal' in origin. Certainly they exercise a powerful influence in attracting viewers. By the end of the twentieth century, they have become a global commodity, with an influence extending well beyond the nation-state (Matelski 1999). That a totally fabricated 'virtual community' can still convey a sense of belonging provides strong prima facie evidence that the cultural work of community does not depend upon physical proximity, as Webber pointed out. The community imagined by Tony Warren in *Coronation Street* was a mocked-up version of a 'traditional' urban working-class community that never existed. It was neither truly working class nor ever truly a community. Action has remained mostly confined to the street itself, which then serves as a kind of stage upon which an endless series of cliffhanging tragicomic plots and sub-plots are enacted and reworked through old and new characters alike. For 'The Street', as for other soaps, there is little or no development, only scene shifts.

Symbolic Communities and the Nature of Belonging

The very constancy of the TV soap opera points to the media's limitations as an institution capable of shaping or supporting realizable social identities. Soap operas reflect primarily the changing times and changing cultures of the societies that make them. From this should one conclude that no purely symbolic community can function as a structuring influence independent of its realization within the specifics of place? Can there ever be community without propinquity? Many have argued that there cannot. Calhoun, for example, has insisted that without face-to-face contact, in what he terms dense multiplex networks, social relationships simply do not meet the criteria to constitute community (Calhoun 1998: 392). Communities of interest, communities based upon a particular identity, Calhoun says, are too one-dimensional to count as 'communal' settings.

Others have argued the opposite, claiming that at the conceptual centre of community is its role as the site of symbolic meaning. According to Andrew Cohen, communities exist to provide meaning, to confer upon us that which makes us human – a cultural identity. The centrality of this symbolic function is revealed all the more clearly by the very 'diminution of the geographical bases of community boundaries' that 'has led to their renewed assertion in symbolic terms' (A. P. Cohen 1989: 117). A similar position is expressed in Benedict Anderson's influential book, *Imagined Communities*, in which he explored the processes that have created a consciousness of national identity amongst peoples (Anderson 1991). He suggests that one of the most significant symbolic functions of communities is to create a sense of belonging amongst people that is capable of being actualized in the absence of direct face-to face social contacts. In contradistinction to Calhoun, Anderson argues that 'imagined communities' based upon a common identification with a nation, race or creed exercise an influence that is in many ways far more profound than that based upon proximal relationships. The war in the former Yugoslavia offers a clear, recent demonstration, when an individual's self-identification as Serb, Croat, Bosnak or Albanian could lead him to kill, rape and pillage his next door neighbours. Although Anderson gives considerable weight to the role of print and the creation of 'linguistic' boundaries that are more socially exclusive than the theologically universal languages of Latin, Arabic and Middle Kingdom Chinese, his account lacks an adequate explanation for the intense emotional attachment that cements a national community, an attachment that is acquired through a wider range of material products than language alone can provide.

If nationalism underlies one prototypical version of a symbolically imagined community, clearly there are many more examples of communities of identity which express a similar level of belongingness and provide a particular meaning to what it is to be 'a man', 'a woman', to be 'black', 'deaf', 'disabled', 'gay', 'mentally ill', 'Muslim' or simply 'cool'. These imagined communities,

or communities of identity, themselves merge into less emotionally intense communities of interest, that depend upon sharing
common pursuits without requiring some intense form of self-
definition. Communities of interest seek to colonize only a part
of the lifeworld, to constitute one element in an individual's social
identity, without placing demands or raising questions about other
roles and other relationships. Football supporters offer a particularly interesting example, as major football clubs have acquired a
global following, and fans of Inter-Milan, Manchester United or
Real Madrid can be found in all corners of the globe. As satellite
TV can broadcast football matches from around the world at
almost any time of day or night, a global following for an inter-
nationally successful club can be supported through nothing more
than access to a TV set, at home or in the local bar, café or pub.
The consequence is a decline in attendance at small-time local
clubs, which languish in the lower divisions of the various national
football leagues and whose support has narrowed to the kind of
support that a school or college football team might expect from
the players' families and friends. For those supporters who are too
frail, too wary or simply too far away to make their way to their
'own' team's stadium, the armchair in the living room offers an
alternative opportunity to participate with a community of
unknown, and scarcely even imagined, supporters. But, for a while,
the viewer can forget the peculiarities of his or her own individual existence and share the anxiety, joy and frustrations of watching his or her own 'self-selected' football club on TV at home. For
a while the virtual community is experienced as real.

Communities of Identity, Coalitions of Interest

The idea of a community based upon identity has continued to
gain in prominence, creating a new politics of difference that is
unlike the earlier politics of class and party. There are four key
sources of identity that have been prominent in establishing a
powerful community of interest amongst their 'members'. These
are race, gender, sexual orientation, and disability. The first in its
power to divide and create agency, undoubtedly, is race and ethnicity. Although the history of ethnic conflict is a long one, specif-

ically racialized conflict based upon identity is of more recent origin, coming to prominence as a division that developments in the post-war welfare state failed to bridge or even to acknowledge (Lewis 2000; Malik 1996). Fuelled by financial globalization and the crumbling legacy of colonialism, peoples with differing languages, customs, habits and appearance now find themselves living side by side, aware of a divide in the conditions of their lives that to many seems impossible to cross.

The second divide is that of sex and gender. Women have found themselves culturally, economically and socially lagging behind the improvements in the conditions of living and the freedoms that men have enjoyed. At the same time they have been enjoined, most often at times of national crisis, to serve as full members of their national communities. As a result, there has been a growing recognition that the divide in status and power between men and women is not reducible to matters of class. The undoubted freedom from the consequences of sexual activity that the contraceptive pill provided has served as an additional impetus, enabling women of child-bearing age to be liberated from unwanted labour, at the same time as increasing their ability to work and play as equals (M. Barrett 1980; McIntosh 1996; Fraser 1997).

A third area of division is around the issue of sexual orientation, which is no longer limited to the binary opposition of heterosexuality versus homosexuality but now includes a multiplicity of existing and emergent identities. These are not only based on gender but have their bases in various sexual desires and practices. The repression that has been a motif of the gay and lesbian population and which engendered a politics of equality has been overtaken by commercial activity as increasingly legal recognition has been gained. This has complicated the nature of identity as issues of incorporation compete with both lifestyles and radicalism (Seidman 1997).

The fourth divide is that between able-bodied and disabled people. In many ways the most complex of all divisions, the political representation of disability has acquired a growing intellectual coherence that has enabled many to challenge the 'naturalness' of the divisions in power, status, influence and resources that exist between the able-bodied and the disabled

(Barnes and Oliver 1995; Marks 1999). But while gender, race and sexual orientation might be thought of as permanent sources of social identity expressed at all points in the lifecourse, disability is not necessarily an invariant feature of an individual's life. Divisions exist between the politics of those with an acquired disability and those congenitally disabled, in terms of the presumed authenticity of their identity. Such divisions, though more marked in the area of disability, present problems to the solidarity of other communities of identity. As a result, doubts have been expressed about the capacity of identity politics to maintain a progressive agenda:

> what [was] politically progressive and open[ed] up new discursive opportunities in the 1970s and 1980s can become a form of closure – and have a repressive value – by the time it is installed as the dominant genre . . . people will use it not because it opens up anything but because they are being spoken by it. (Grossberg 1996: 88)

Writers in the Cultural Studies tradition seek to 'relocate' the discourse of identity, 'beyond models of oppression' toward 'a model of articulation as transformative practice, as a singular becoming of a community' (Grossberg 1996: 88). If the communities of identity created by the Sixties' social movements prove not to be the 'right' sort of communities, it remains unclear how they can 'move on' toward more transformative practices. Communities of identity are defined not just by those who are included within them but also by their distinction from the 'general' community. Communities of identity seek to cement the bonds within them, defining identity as much by exclusion as by inclusion – defining a diffuse 'other' who inhabits the amorphous spaces that constitute the broader community.

By contrast, communities of interest provide less exclusionary social movements. Appearing somewhat later than the social movements built around race, gender, sexual orientation and disability, these associations have sought to identify common ground around themes of general social protest – ecology movements, animal rights groups, and movements concerned with particular issues such as factory farming, transport policies, or particular urban or rural developments – that are broadly lumped together as 'issue politics'. Though tending to focus upon matters that relate to a specific time and a specific place, these new communities or coalitions of interest contain a membership that extends beyond those of communities defined by neighbourhood, class, ethnicity, age or gender, forming what Georgio Agambe has called a community of 'singularity'. A community of singularity consists of nothing more than the relationships it sustains between its members. It is a community reduced to a state of 'belonging in itself', a point which leads us to our final theme: namely, community as the extent of belongingness in a society.

The Community of Communities: Theorizing Social Capital

After the Second World War, the powerful conflicts between the classes seemed to have been bridged, and the prospect of a more inclusive, solidaristic and yet liberal and prosperous nation-state seemed on the point of being realized. But the politics of identity disrupted this social democratic consensus, opening up new divides in areas which previously had been naturalized (e.g. around race, gender, sexual orientation and disability). The failure to resolve these conflicts, as well as the methods used to try to resolve them, have created new concerns over the apparent decline in people's sense of belonging. The problem of community in the aftermath of the Sixties has been formulated not so much in terms of a disappearing community, but as the disappearance of something more intangible, the very 'feeling' of community.

The Sixties' cultural revolution did much to switch the focus of community away from spatialized communities and neighbourhood solidarities to personal identities and the struggle for recognition amongst the all too visible members of 'invisible' communities. But within this new community of communities something seemed lacking. That missing ingredient began to be identified as the absence of 'social capital'. If the idea of the new, post-war, post-Sixties society was to be a community of communities, something was needed to contain these communities of interest and identity to prevent the dissolution of the broader community of association (Tönnies' *Gesellschaft*). Society, as a whole, needed to shore up its own social capital, its sense of general belongingness. In his book, *Bowling Alone*, Putnam credited the sociologist James Coleman with putting the term 'social capital' 'firmly and finally on the intellectual agenda in the late 1980s', although others, including Putnam himself, have clearly contributed to establishing its credentials as a popular social-scientific concept (Putnam 2001: 19–20).

Amongst the various definitions and formulations of social capital that have been proposed, it is possible to identify three central elements: one relating to the size and weight of people's social networks (how large, how intensive, how robust), the second relating to the normative values of reciprocity attached to those networks (how much trust and belongingness), and the third relating to the role of these networks as 'bonds' or 'bridges' between individual actors ('bridges' are horizontal networks that cut across vertical divisions such as class, while 'bonds' are vertical networks that separate groups, organizations or families from each other). High social capital is characterized by extensive social networks, which form bridges between groups and which express a strong sense of reciprocity and trust. It is considered to be constitutive of an effective integrated and productive society.

Putnam vacillates between treating social capital as a personal attribute – the extensiveness and depth of individual social actors' ties with each other – and as a quality of a society or nation-state – the overall extent of civic engagement and the size and effectiveness of informal and voluntary associations within the broader society. This duality is reflected in Calhoun's earlier delineation of community as being both a bounded arena or social field and a set of social relationships or bonds, possessing varying degrees of 'community-ness' (Calhoun 1980: 117). The question of whether the individual or the community exemplify 'social capital' is at bottom unanswerable. Treating community as a variable, which is how the term 'social capital' is used, leads inevitably to the examination of individual consciousness (people's reported sense of trust/belongingness) and individual actions (people's reported frequency of participation in communal events). It would seem that there can be no such thing as social capital without individual social capitalists.

The issue for Putnam and for other 'communitarians' is not what defines a community (the delineation of its identity), but what defines the extent of community (its social capital). As we have seen, 'identity' raises the question of both spatial and symbolic forms of community and what constitute the markers or boundaries of belonging. The aftermath of the 1960s' cultural revolution can be seen as having replaced a strongly localized sense of belonging based upon propinquity, kinship and attachment to a broader occupational community with a much looser, more personalized sense of identity that relies more upon imagined communities of interest than upon the everyday material interchanges of work and neighbourhood. 'Social capital' also raises the question of belongingness, but its focus is upon the intensiveness and extensiveness of that belongingness itself, irrespective of the form of the community to which one belongs.

As Putnam recognizes, social capital or belongingness retains a degree of ambiguity as regards its status as a social good. This ambiguity seems to be a constant accompaniment to all formulations of 'community' within the social sciences. It is as central a problem within Modernity 2 as it was in Modernity 1. Strong forms of community and high levels of social capital create powerful social networks based upon widespread norms of reciprocity and a selective intensification of social identities. These foster resilience and an enhanced communal ability to cope with longstanding adverse circumstances, producing lower rates of individual malaise and demoralization. For those who lack alternative personal, social or emotional capital, the benefits of belonging to high social capital communities may be particularly important. Equally, communities that express very limited norms of reciprocity, which are not capable of sustaining any strong pooling of identities, and which offer very limited guidelines on the value and appropriateness of different lifestyles may adapt more readily and more effectively to change by tolerating greater personal freedoms and supporting greater individual diversity. There again, the costs of low levels of social capital may be more widespread individual malaise and morbidity, particularly amongst those who have less access to other forms of capital.

The problem with community is a matter not simply of its definition and measurement, but also of its continuing ambivalent social worth within a modernized world economy. As globaliza-tion promotes further blurring of social identities and the contin-uing destabilization of the institutional organization of time and space, calls to combat this process emerge on both the Left and the Right of the political spectrum. The Left protests the growing power of a rootless capital that is free to roam the world follow-ing its own whims and dictates. The Right protests the decline in law and order and the fostering of a global underclass encircling civic society. Both appeal, for different reasons and in different ways, to a global class of situated 'vagabonds' (Bauman 2000), those most bound to their place in the world and least able to benefit from reductions in the power and influence of the local community. Where once the most mobile in society formed its underclass, the beggars and vagabonds excluded from modernity's feast, the socially excluded of Modernity 2 are drawn from those most rooted in their community, communities that are singularly disconnected from the other circuits and benefits of capital. As was the case with the beggars of early modernity, amongst the vagabonds left behind in the marginal communities of post-industrial society are the aged poor.

Expanding Communities, Declining Solidarities

The nature of community and the sociological understanding thereof have undergone a systematic transformation, both in what it is, where it is, and how it has been studied. Once 'community' referred to a solidaristic totalizing community, where the divisions of class, gender and generation were managed with minimal con-flict by the overarching dominance of a settled and established way of life, where everyone had their place, and only the ill, the odd and the unfit moved out. The dominating influence of the community, commune or parish over the life and times of people living under this 'old regime' has no doubt been exaggerated, but the structures of the traditional community provided for all in their own way. Those deemed aged and infirm were recognized as a communal responsibility, even when family members were on hand, and when family members were unable to cope with the consequences of their relatives' aged infirmity, the resources of the parish or commune would be extended to address such contingencies. That those resources were often not sufficient may be true; that some old people lived and died in quite pitiful conditions is a matter of record; but during those times the poor were a large and demographically amorphous group whose status became 'a problem' only when they left behind 'their community' to become shiftless beggars and vagabonds, for whom neither the local nor the national authorities had much time.

Industrialization and urbanization led to a steady process of internal migration. In the absence of the benign but patriarchal influence of parish or commune, the urban neighbourhoods in which an increasing proportion of the population now found themselves offered much less in the way of official sources of comfort. As we have shown, by the end of the nineteenth century, if they could not work and earn, many older people faced the prospect of institutionalization and/or impoverishment as families were less and less able to support extended generations from their own wages. This adversity was ameliorated by the introduction of old age pensions. Inter-generational solidarity was further reinforced by the general improvement in family [household] income during the late nineteenth and early twentieth centuries. Between 1860 and 1915, a growing number of men and women aged 65 and over lived in households that they shared with extended family. This resulted, in some communities at least, in almost every other person aged 65 and over living with extended kin. In others, rather less than one in four people over 65 did so (see Ruggles 1987: appendix F). For those who did live on their own or as an elderly couple, their sons, daughters, daughters-in-law and grandchildren would generally live in close proximity, either in the same block or, if not, within easy walking distance. The urban neighbourhood became a site where family ties were embedded as much as, if not more than, traditions of 'neighbouring'. From the latter part of the nineteenth century up until the Second World War, most men over sixty worked; most women over sixty kept house or helped keep house. These worlds, of home, work and the local neighbourhood, though powerfully structured by class and gender, were shared, by and large, across the generations.

The generational field of Modernity 1 was cemented by the bonds created by corporate society – Tönnies' *burgerliche gesell-*

schaft. The social compact between the classes and the generations nevertheless contained the seeds of its own demise. The bureaucratic individualization that was intended to strengthen and unify the citizenry of the nation-state created generational schisms that caused the old communities of place to be increasingly overshadowed by the new communities of identity and personal interest. Inter-generational social mobility rose steadily throughout the twentieth century, levelling off only recently, and then primarily for men (Payne and Roberts 2002; Vallet 1999). Those growing up in the 1960s have continued by and large to do well, many leaving behind the social, cultural and geographical spaces that their parents and grandparents occupied. As members of these birth cohorts reach retirement in the twenty-first century, their experience of later life is increasingly distant from the communities and neighbourhoods where previous generations had spent their later life.

Cut off from the solidarities of class, the constancies of a local community, and the inter-generational connectedness that their parents and grandparents once experienced, this new cohort of retirees seem less well capitalized socially, culturally and emotionally than previous generations, despite being materially so much better off. Can symbolic communities offer the same level of support and belonging that the spatialized communities of the earlier twentieth century did? In the context of the greater material capital of those now in their fifties and sixties, do they need to? If the wider communal identities of class and nation no longer find expression in the social spaces of the locality, what holds the generations together? Is the future a society of age-gated communities, where social inclusion is purchased at the cost of liquidating a lifetime of accumulated social capital? What choices exist for retired people to exercise agency and express their own sense of belonging by choosing to resist 'ageing in place'? And finally, what of those who cannot choose, who can do no other than grow old in place – what future fourth-age community do they risk being assigned to, the latter-day vagabonds of Modernity 2? In the next chapter, we shall attempt answers to these questions, before addressing the broader question of where, if anywhere, within a globalized community of singularity, age now figures.

7

Community in Later Life

Living a long time has commonly meant living a long time in one place. The longer an individual lives, the less likely he or she is to move. Hence, community (in the sense of a geographically located structure) has tended to be an important source of continuity and coherence to the individual lifecourse as people grow older. Whatever meanings are attributed to later life, whether through the moral organization of the lifecourse or simply through the roles that are expected of a person at certain ages, stable communities rarely present problems (and equally rarely offer choices) in developing and supporting a social identity for 'age'. It could also be added that this is equally true for gender, ethnicity or class. Traditionally, communities sustain, rather than challenge, statuses.

The industrialization and urbanization of the late nineteenth century produced far-reaching changes in the ordering of society. The mediating social structures binding together an individual's past, present and future were no longer the exclusive preserve of the village, the neighbourhood or the family. The state and the market introduced alternative sources of identity and of status. Through the process of 'institutionalized individualization',[1] the state began to establish many of the key institutions that came both to define the various phases of the modern lifecourse and to manage the transitions between them. As affluence spread across class, gender and age strata during the course of the twentieth century, these institutionalized stages or phases of the lifecourse became more open to commodification within and *outside* the labour market, principally through the rise of mass consumption. Age became segmented by market forces – fostering a gradual 'de-institutionalization' of the lifecourse (Kohli and Rein 1991: 21–2).

This hyper-commodification of the lifecourse forms part of a broader trend toward what Habermas has called the 'colonization of the lifeworld', whereby more and more aspects of life are brought into focus and made salient by people's activities as consumers. As Bauman has pointed out, 'consumer conduct . . . [has] move[d] steadily into the position of [being] the cognitive and moral focus of life, the integrative bond of the society and the focus of systemic management' (Bauman 1991: 49). This process affects equally those in the work-force as well as those who are out of (or not yet in) it. As a result, many of the structures that organized the modern lifecourse have been transformed. Community is no exception.

From the old regime's 'one-class' rural parishes to the class-conscious differentiated urban neighbourhoods of the early twentieth century, spatial boundaries and physical proximity remained central to the sense of community. Then, as the identities and positions fashioned by these localized spaces became insufficiently flexible to accommodate the changing nature of post-war society, new forms of community emerged. The roots of these new communities lay less in the unalterable physicality of place and more in the realm of the symbolic – the 'imagined' community. In the wake of the 1960s cultural revolution, new forms of collective identity 'seemed to be displacing class-based political mobilisation in Western Europe . . . changing dominant normative and cultural codes by gaining recognition for [these] new identities' (Polletta and Jasper 2001: 286). These new social movements privileged the symbolic over the spatial community. Where previous cohorts had mobilized around class or drawn their sense of identity and solidarity from 'kinship' within the local community, participants and fellow-travellers within the new social movements expressed their collective identity through the imagined communities of race, ethnicity, gender, sexual orientation and disability. Political demands were increasingly represented as demands for greater personal freedom, which evolved into a heightened concern over individual rights and relationships (Weeks 2000: 181). Issues of identity became anchored in lifestyle; and as lifestyles proliferated, they were sustained and amplified by progressive market segmentation (L. Cohen 2003: 292–344; Slater 1997: 190–3).

After the collapse of the Bretton Woods' agreement, it became clear that neither national governments nor national markets could guarantee unending personal and economic progress. As individual vice came to profit over collective virtue, the price of the continuing cultural diversification of life seemed to be growing social inequality. A globalizing market and a globalizing culture threatened to steamroller through the boundaries of all the 'old' communities. Within this de-regulated society, where identity seems to be a matter of personal choice, greater choice is accompanied by a greater sense of risk. Collective concerns were voiced during the 1960s about the disappearance of community's normative boundaries, but many of these were dismissed at the time as the reactionary forces of a pre-war society resisting the cultural changes of a new youthful society. In more recent times, that concern has generalized to fears that the very *idea* of community is on the point of disappearing from the collective consciousness.[2]

In this risky and ungrounded world, the choices of later life can seem to be confined to choosing between two equally mythical forms of 'community': an aspirational heaven or an actual hell. Retirees can either realize their later life within a post-industrial, hyper-individualized and potentially illusionary 'third age' community, with the attendant criticism of selfishness, greed, false consciousness and the squandering of all sources of capital, or they can decline to act, staying in the same place and risking ageing alone as the old communities of class, kinship and neighbourhood slowly dissolve. According to Francis Fukuyama:

> [T]he older person of the early twenty first century . . . will pass his or her waning years living alone in a house or apartment visited occasionally by a son or a daughter who are themselves past retirement age and seeking ways to deal with their own deteriorating health. The connection with these relatives will be tenuous because the long and tumultuous personal lives they led when younger . . . have left their descendants with a sentimental but slightly detached relationship. . . . Life has become completely de-ritualized. The different transitions from one phase of life to another are not marked by familiar and comforting ceremonies that connect the individual to generations past and those yet to come but are rather a matter of improvisation. The ability to innovate

and remake oneself which had seemed like such a valuable characteristic in early phases of life now leads only to incredible loneliness. The end when it comes is faced alone. (Fukuyama 1999: 120)

Roots, Propinquity and Ageing in Place

Perhaps the first, if not the best, place to start is the matter of rootedness. The longer people live, the less they move. Preference for one's own neighbourhood increases as the costs of moving come to outweigh the benefits. There appears to be a growing desire to stay put. This attachment to place, this wish to stay rooted, leads many older people to experience the mixed blessings of staying on in a home that they furnished decades earlier for a family who will have left home before they themselves reach retirement (Hancock et al. 1999).

The social, occupational and residential mobility of successive cohorts of young people has led to weaker links between the generations. Jobs in the expanding service sector have diminished the importance of geographically based occupational communities. The traditional 'proletarian' communities (Lockwood 1966) based around particular work places no longer play as much of a role in embedding labour within society. The inter-generational transmission of work and domestic culture that characterized the generational field of Modernity 1 has disappeared, reducing the sense of community between and within kinship groups (Pooley and Turnbull 1998). Rather than gaining in resources as a result of continuing residence in the same area, people who stay and age are likely to find themselves less able to draw upon the local community as the local community itself becomes less resourceful, accessible and meaningful after kith and kin have gone. Removed from the labour market and from the world of work through retirement and with more limited contacts with working family members, older people may find access to and engagement with the wider social world more difficult as they 'age in place' while others respond to the market and move on.

This is a situation that confronts those least well-off in terms of social, material and physical assets – retired people dependent upon state benefits, without independent sources of wealth or income of their own, and without access to significant family resources. Unable to do otherwise than 'age in place', they risk a future when they can no longer resist being bussed into the ascribed communities of 'the fourth age'. As Crow and Allan (1995) have noted, communities operate within particular time frameworks. Alongside the problems of 'ageing in place', there is also the ageing of places, which is not just a matter of 'local history'. The transformations in the social composition of neighbourhoods, their changing spatial boundaries, and the disappearance of sites of previous symbolic significance like the local pub or the local shop may render them less and less familiar to those who have chosen, or are compelled, to 'age in place'.

Ageing and Mobility

How much empirical support is there for such sweeping generalities? Studies of mobility have generally found that adult residential mobility declines with age.[3] This pattern of lifecourse mobility has been observed at least since the eighteenth century (Pooley and Turnbull 1998: 205), when many of the restrictions on the freedom of labour to move were lifted. Although this pattern has remained quite constant over time, the absolute amount of population movement, as well as the distances moved, has increased over time (Pooley and Turnbull 1998: 207). Only in the twentieth century did retirement became an important reason for those over 60 to move, and even then such moves made up less than 10 per cent of all migration throughout most of this period.

Unsurprisingly, then, the early view of gerontologists was that older people were 'neighbourhood bound' (Cantor 1975). The notion of rootedness in old age that was promoted in this earlier gerontological literature reflected an ambiguity towards old age that has long characterized studies of old age. On the one hand, such rootedness has been represented as a reflection of older people's characterological rigidity and reluctance to change their ways. On the other hand, it has been used to argue that old people constitute the 'roots' of communities – key elements of solidarity and continuity in a changing world. Assumptions about the dependency of older people on their neighbourhoods continue to be expressed, and much is still made of their 'ageing in place' (Oh 2003). While this rootedness is sometimes treated as a virtue, with the implication that 'remaining in the community' represents successful resistance to a potentially enforced relocation into a 'Home', it can equally be viewed as a reflection of age-related disability – restricted mobility resulting from a lack of both symbolic and material capital.

A countervailing perspective can be discerned, which suggests that older people are neither disengaged from, nor structurally dependent upon, their neighbourhood. 'Modern' retirees, it is claimed, express and exercise a positive desire to travel, to see other places, and in doing so, enjoy the possibility to choose an alternative place and style of retirement that suits and pleases them (Stallmann and Espinoza 1996). Such choices do not negate 'ageing in place', but they convert staying in one's home into a positive choice rather than the consequence of an inability to choose. In short, they represent agency within the community.

This latter perspective is exemplified in the research into retirement migration that began in the late 1970s and early 1980s in the USA (Walters 2002; Walters and Wilder 2003). This research interest was fuelled by the fact that retirement was occurring at earlier ages and was accompanied by rising wealth and income. Consequently, more and more people began to consider moving at the point of retirement (Warnes 1993). Some of these moves were seasonal and involved buying or renting a second home, while others were permanent. Both seasonal and permanent migration typically involves a move to a warmer climate. Free of the ties of work and family, and without ill health limiting their choices, retired people began to reduce their 'attachment to place' and head for the sun (see fig. 7.1). For every retired person or couple who did move, there were many more who were actively contemplating such moves (Fokkema, Gierveld and Nijkamp 1996). Such desires do not mean that the majority of retired people want to leave the homes they have lived in during their working life. The strength of social bonds, as well as attachment to their own homes and possessions, still play a large part in influencing decisions to stay or move (Ekerdt et al. 2003). But movement and the freedom to move have become possibilities that contrast with the short-term moves of earlier periods. Those

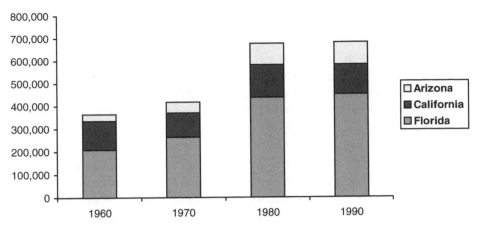

Figure 7.1   Numbers of people aged 60+ moving to the US sun belt states, 1960–90. Source: Haas and Serow 2002: 160, table 4.

were moves governed not by desire but by the varying family fortunes and health crises imposed on a population who mostly rented rather than owned the place where they were living (Rogers 1988; Warnes 1993).

Not only has residential mobility increased amongst the retired population, but the number of dual residencies has also grown. This has led, in North America, to the emergence, within the retired population, of 'snowbirds' and 'snowflakes'. These refer to retired people living in the colder, more northerly states of the USA and Canada who buy or rent property in the sunshine belt of the USA (typically Arizona, California, the Carolinas and Florida), where they spend some (snowflakes) or all (snowbirds) of their winters. Similar patterns of seasonal migration are evident in Australia, where the preferred 'winter' destination is Queensland's gold coast (Stimpson et al. 1996; Mings 1997). In Europe, the numbers of 'snowbirds' are also rising. British, German, Swiss and Swedish retirees are buying second homes in southern Europe, Spain particularly, but also Italy, Malta and Portugal (King, Warnes and Williams 1988; Gustafson 2001). Even if the majority of older people do not leave home for good, a steadily increasing number are engaging in seasonal migration both in

America and in Europe. A new 'life cycle' pattern of international holiday travel has become evident, where rates peak during young adulthood, before child rearing and work tie people down until early retirement, and then rise again after child rearing and work are over (Collins and Tisdell 2000, 2002).

Do these phenomena represent improving mobility with age – new freedoms from the ties binding older people to their neighbourhood, new possibilities of not being tied down by age and agedness? Is there a parallel with the earlier 'release' of working people from the ties of the land, during the eighteenth century, that set in train a massive process of rural to urban migration and which led eventually to the wholesale transformation of society? Just as the beneficiaries of that earlier, double-edged freedom to sell one's labour took on an iconic status, in the aspirations of a new 'aristocracy of labour', so might the beneficiaries of this new retirement mobility serve as exemplary 'silver-agers' poised to transform the chilly landscape of later life. Using their deferred income to purchase the amenities of a warm and well-provided-for lifestyle, more exciting and empowering later-life communities may emerge to offer a new take on 'ageing in place'.

The destination, rather than the point of departure, defines the pattern of 'amenity' retirement migration. The sites for retirement mirror the sites chosen for holidays, places where the year-round climate is good, where leisure facilities are plentiful, and where retirees are likely to find significant numbers of like-minded people in comparable circumstances (Newbold 1995). The beneficial consequences of this development are not confined to retirees. As the receiving communities gain access to the surplus that the retirees bring with them, the golden glow of the retirement sun belt takes on a distinctly material reality for all (Deller 1995; Hodge 1991). These positive benefits encompass a gradually widening range of locations, 'as the servicing of rural areas with basic utilities, transport and telecommunications has improved and as the income and assets of successive cohorts reaching retirement age has risen' (Warnes 1993: 464). Improved public transport and increased car ownership contributed to this dispersion. The reduction in the cost of air travel has increased international amenity migration. Retirement has begun, like tourism before it, to extend across a wider range of countries and continents, adding a new 'retirement' dimension to the globalization of cultures and commerce (Warnes 2001).

Of course, such agency is structured. Retired international and inter-state migrants are certainly not a random sample of retirees. Better-educated and from predominantly professional, managerial or *petit bourgeois* backgrounds, these migrating retirees possess above-average levels of income and wealth (Rodriguez, Fernandez-Mayoralas and Rojo 1998; Walters 2000). While the average person in Europe, Australia or North America does not routinely choose to undertake long-distance residential moves upon retirement, those more able to afford to are most likely to do so. At the other extreme, the poorest people in society are least likely to move from the place where they have spent most of their working life, at least not until they are moved into care or have their children move in with them.[4] It is the 'poor' who are most likely to 'age in place', whose dependency upon their neighbourhood will bring them mixed benefits. Though some no doubt benefit from the protection and support of the 'old' neighbourhood, many find themselves exposed to their own individual ageing frailties, reflected ever more mercilessly in the eyes of their unknown and uncaring neighbours. It is not so much the increased risk of actual victimization that poor old people face in seriously disadvantaged communities so much as the spectre of their vulnerability and helplessness to control those risks (Fokkema, Gierveld and Nijkamp 1996: 354).

Ageing and the Neighbourhood

Not every retiree who ages in place perceives their neighbourhood negatively, neither do people necessarily 'age' at a faster rate as a result of staying put in their community. Living in a pleasant neighbourhood with family and friends close by, with good local services and reasonable access to a range of leisure facilities, clearly suits many people, who feel neither powerless, vulnerable nor oppressed by their age. Longino and his colleagues compared levels of satisfaction of Florida amenity migrant retirees (who had chosen *not* to age in place) with those of Minnesotan retirees matched for social background who had chosen to 'age in place'.

They found that both groups reported high levels of satisfaction, which led the authors to conclude that '[p]erhaps the greatest advantages of living in some place, the reasons for wanting to live there, are constructions drawn around oneself to justify the residence . . . (and) perhaps these perceptions grow up after the fact for most persons who move or do not move' (Longino, Perzynski and Stoller 2002: 48). Their point – that people's judgements of the satisfactoriness of their neighbourhood or community are primary in determining their well-being – raises several questions, not least the role that the actual structure of a community or neighbourhood plays in influencing quality of life in retirement. Are communities of place, first and foremost, communities of consciousness, no less imaginary than the imagined communities of identity?

Studies of the impact of the neighbourhood on the lives of its inhabitants go back to the 1930s, when they formed a key theme in the urban sociology of the Chicago School. But early urban sociology was concerned with delineating the neighbourhood and its impact upon the character and psychological world of its inhabitants. The focus was particularly upon young people and predicated upon the potentially 'baleful' influence of street life. They were most interested in the moral and psychological impact of city life, and its role in contributing to delinquency or madness. Its impact on later life was scarcely addressed. Subsequent, post-war British community studies did focus upon age and inter-generational relationships, but their emphasis was upon a 'thick' description of the lives led by older people within their communities. Their moral stance was based upon the positive role played by the neighbourhood in providing a source of contact, support and comfort to older people and actively maintaining the ties between the generations (Townsend 1963; Willmott and Young 1971; Young and Willmott 1962). Whilst pre- and post-war US sociology viewed urban neighbourhoods as potential threats to the moral order, UK community studies saw the neighbourhood as a bulwark of that order (Frankenberg 1966).

More recently, attempts have been made to assess the role of community as a 'structuring' structure, with a potential to influence for good or ill the health and well-being of those who live there. To demonstrate such 'neighbourhood influence' on 'age related' outcomes, it is necessary to show that these effects operate in ways that cannot more parsimoniously be ascribed to the characteristics of the person (such as their age, gender, income, education, beliefs and attitudes toward their community) rather than the neighbourhood itself. For example, neighbourhoods with the greatest structural disadvantages may preferentially attract and retain those least able to exercise independent agency. Individuals who are more resourceful may move out, or establish links with alternative communities that minimize the importance of the neighbourhood. Likewise, neighbourhoods with many positive attributes may attract people with pre-existing advantages who will be in a better position to buy their way into such areas. Such a person–environment fit would not matter if there was a general tendency for most people to think that the neighbourhood where they live is a good place to live simply because it is where they themselves live. If that were so, then, following Longino et al.'s supposition, one might expect that 'neighbourhood effects' are nothing more than subjective expressions of a generalized 'contentment'; happy people being happy to live in the place they happen to live in, and unhappy people unhappy to live wherever.

Studies focusing on 'satisfaction' with one's neighbourhood, or subjective reports about the quality of one's neighbourhood have consistently shown that older people (or older cohorts) rate their neighbourhood more positively than do younger people. This general tendency of older people to value their neighbourhood is moderated, to some degree, by the type of neighbourhood in which they live and how long they have lived there. Most retired people living in social housing, surrounded by large families and/or younger, single-person households, view their neighbourhood less positively than those living in privately owned housing in high-income areas.[5] Nevertheless, the general trend toward higher expressed levels of satisfaction with one's neighbourhood amongst older people cannot be considered sufficient evidence that 'ageing in place' has no harmful effects.

So we have to turn to those relatively few studies that have tried to examine the impact of neighbourhood quality on indicators of an individual's 'third' or 'fourth' age status, such as levels of disability, chronic illness and emotional well-being, that are independent of the individual's own subjective judgements. While we do not wish to reduce the third age to a set of individual attributes of fitness and health, such attributes are relevant, as they render the social world of the third age more accessible. Some recent studies suggest that neighbourhoods can exercise such effects. In the Americans' Changing Lives study (Balfour and Kaplan 2002), much of the poorer health status of older black Americans could be explained by the different community contexts in which black and white older Americans live. In one of the longest-running longitudinal studies of health and illness in the USA, the Alameda County study, researchers concluded that:

> poor quality neighbourhood environments are associated with increased loss of physical function in older adults [such that] after adjusting for many individual and demographic characteristics the risk of overall functional loss among people who report multiple serious neighbourhood problems is more than twice that of those who report no serious neighbourhood problems. (Balfour and Kaplan 2002: 512)

This is a particularly powerful finding, because the study was looking at episodes of disability arising in older people who were fit when they entered the study. Because of its prospective design, the research was less likely to confound the structuring effect of the neighbourhood with the structured effect of people's own 'ageing', a flaw that blighted earlier cross-sectional studies which tried to establish causal links between neighbourhood effects, perceived health, extent of co-morbidity (i.e. multiple health problems) and levels of disability (Atkinson and Kintrea 2001).

Health and fitness represent one parameter facilitating access to a third age style of later life. Neighbourhoods exercise an even more direct influence upon social participation, through factors such as transport links, housing, local public amenities and local leisure resources. The lack of such neighbourhood resources creates obstacles to engagement with the broader social world (e.g. people not leaving their houses through a fear of crime). That the environment can play an important part in creating 'the good

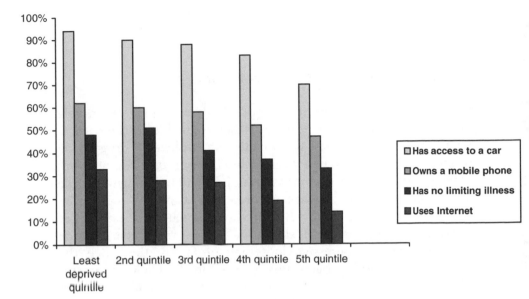

Figure 7.2 Individual access to selected third age resources by level of neighbourhood deprivation. Source: English Longitudinal Study on Ageing, unpublished data supplied by Martin Hyde, Research Fellow with the ELSA study group, University College London, 2004.

life in old age' is, as Wahl and Weisman (2003) have pointed out, 'current, readable and persuasive'. According to the 'environmental docility' hypothesis, increasing age leads to increasing vulnerability to the impact of one's environment. Living in an environment with poor transport, few shops, a deteriorating housing stock, and high rates of street crime might well be expected to impact adversely upon retired people, conveying them into old age more rapidly than the warm sun and the blue skies of Florida or the Mediterranean coast. Some illustration of these effects can be found in figure 7.2, based upon data concerning fitness, activity and 'engagement' of people aged between 60 and 74 in the English Longitudinal Study of Ageing (ELSA). As the figure shows, those who live in the most deprived neighbourhoods also have the least access to some of the key resources for participating in third age culture (in this instance, good health, personal transport, ease of communication and Internet 'connectivity').

Neighbourhood and the Proximity of Kin

Communities of propinquity are not constituted, however, merely out of bricks and concrete; nor are they reducible to their transport links, telephone networks, or the ambient level of drug taking or street crime. Central to the idea of community is the network of social relationships that provide support and meaning to people as socially constituted beings. A core element in such social relation network is the family. Research on the nature of family ties in later life is extensive. Most of the evidence from that research demonstrates a progressive loosening of family ties since the 1950s. This trend has been most marked in the USA and north-western Europe, but family ties are loosening across most of Europe (Vogel 2003: 406–8). Two key factors emerge in this loosening of family connections that shed light on understanding the impact of community upon later life. The first is the change in closeness between older parents (mothers especially) and their adult children (daughters especially) arising from less frequent joint living arrangements and greater physical distances between parents and their adult children. The second factor is the general change in the nature of kinship and contacts between kin, which rely less upon physical proximity but instead depend upon looser, more flexible systems of 'keeping in touch'.

As both Townsend, and Young and Willmott, pointed out some time ago, 'traditional' working-class neighbourhoods were marked not so much by the quality of neighbourly relationships as by the presence of kin living within the same neighbourhood (Townsend 1963; Young and Willmott 1962; Willmott and Young 1971). Family relationships and community relationships were intimately connected. Central to these connections was the relationship between mothers and their daughters. By the end of the nineteenth century, most Western societies were well on the way to becoming urban societies. Universal male suffrage had been achieved. There was steady progress toward establishing a family wage that provided sufficient income for a man to maintain his

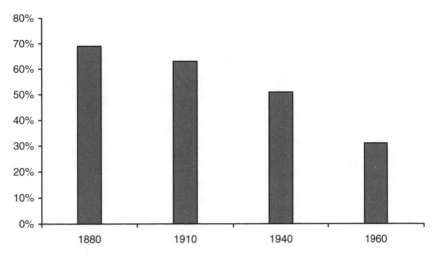

Figure 7.3 Percentage of elderly US women living with their children, 1880–1960. Source: adapted from Ruggles 1993: table 3.

wife and children at home, as well as saving something for emergencies and still having some spare cash for luxuries such as tobacco, alcohol and entertainment. The social world of the working class established in Modernity 1 was powerfully gendered; work took men out of their neighbourhood – to the factory, office, mine or building site – leaving the women behind to mind the home and maintain the community.[6]

Throughout the first half of the twentieth century, few married women returned to work after raising their children. Instead, they remained at home, where their ties to neighbourhood and family continued to grow, incorporating an ever wider range of kin relations. As they grew older, women became ever more closely connected to their community, unlike their men, who tended to have progressively weaker links with their community as they grew older. Most ageing women who could lived with their kin in a pattern that had been established over many generations. Comparing the number of mothers of middle-aged children who were still alive with the numbers who were living with their middle-aged children, Ruggles (1993) has shown that nearly all (over 90 per cent) of the mothers of middle-aged children still alive in 1880 lived with their children. Even by 1940, the figure was still over 50 per cent. By 1960, however, co-residence between adult children and their ageing parents had dropped to less than 30 per cent, and by 1980 it was a mere 12.5 per cent. Between 1880 and 1940, over half of US women aged 65 and over (married and widowed, with and without children) lived together with at least one or other of their children (see fig. 7.3 above).

Much of the work of community was women's work, and many of the ties that constituted community were ties based upon kinship rather than neighbourly relations. Young and Willmott (1962) pointed out the contrasts that were emerging in mother–daughter relationships in their comparative study of an English working-class neighbourhood and a middle-class suburb in the post-war period:

> In the one, mothers and daughters are each other's constant companions and helpmates. In the other the same bond is there in affection and in the care and support that daughters give their mothers . . . in their advancing years. But it is by and large less important . . . because the relationship of husband and wife matters more. (Young and Willmott 1962: 70)

This shift from parent to partner, that Willmott and Young first observed in England's middle-class suburbs, spread across most social groups, with the notable exception of minority ethnic communities where mother–daughter ties have remained powerful (De Vos and Arias 2003). Given sufficient financial independence, most older and younger people now prefer to maintain independent households. Devine has argued that working-class and middle-class families experience the same desire for independence. In the past, she suggests, parents and their adult children lived together out of necessity rather than choice, maintaining independent households whenever they were in a position to do so (Devine 1992: 72–3). Co-residence of mothers and daughters has declined in proportion to each others' own improving economic status.

The greater financial independence that parents and their adult children have experienced seems to have changed permanently the nature of community and kinship (McGarry and Schoeni

2000). But is the decline in mother–daughter co-residency a key factor in the decline of the local community? Have these weaker community ties contributed to the marginalization of older women, a marginalization achieved through the separation that younger women have achieved from their own mothers? Do older people who still live with their children benefit or suffer from their co-residency? Are the effects the same today as they were in the past? Such questions are not easily answered. Attitudes and expectations about adult child–parent relationships have undergone many changes. Family life in Modernity 2 seems to have acquired a different set of meanings and positionalities. Given the value placed upon living independently in retirement, it is plausible that current retirees who find themselves living with their children risk compromising their status as third agers, either through reduced autonomy, constant unfavourable age–status comparisons, or through infantilization of the older parent by the adult children.

Support for such a possibility comes from longitudinal studies of closeness to kin, which indicate that those who are fitter, younger and wealthier in later life tend to move away from their children over time, while those who are disabled, older and/or poorer tend to move closer (Silverstein 1995). While it is true that most retired people maintain close relationships with their children, there is considerable difference between living with, or living in the same apartment or street, and living in two different localities, even if they are only a few miles away. The decline in co-residence means that neighbourhood no longer constitutes a social network based upon the gendered interconnection between the generations. More and more, it is an environment characterized by 'sparsely knit, loosely bounded, frequently changing networks' (Phillipson et al. 1999: 741). But, despite the decline in proximity and consequent loosening of neighbourhood ties, links between the generations have not changed dramatically. Indeed, they may be becoming more extensive as a result of widening car ownership amongst parents and children, the near universal availability of the telephone and more extensive kinship networks, including networks that include a widening circle of step-children and step-grandchildren (Le Gall and Martin 1997). The paradox is that as family relationships have become separated from communal relationships, the latter have become attenuated, while the former exhibit new, and potentially more vital, forms of exchange. Families find ways to stay in touch without the mixed benefits of co-residency or close neighbourhood proximity. Within these changing relationships, it is possible to observe greater equality in the exchange of support, more opportunities for parents to maintain a balanced system of exchange with their adult children and at the same time sustain an independent lifestyle (Vollenwyder et al. 2002).

Communities of Identity and Common Interests in Later Life

As a result of higher income, increased mobility, and looser and more extensive family ties, there has been a clear trend for the local community, the neighbourhood, to function as a much less salient structure in the lives of young and old alike. While retired people's ties to poor-quality neighbourhoods may result in their being socially and functionally more aged and disabled than would otherwise be the case, the potential benefits conferred upon those choosing to move to more pleasant communities in which to enjoy their retirement are less clearly established. In many ways, amenity retirement migration might seem to promise most, particularly to those who see retirement as 'the longest holiday you never had'. But it seems to engender, in researchers perhaps more than in retirees, a degree of discomfort.

One senses an undercurrent of reprobation, as if the journey to Arizona or the Costa Del Sol involves turning one's back on the real world of class, kin, conflict and contemporary culture – all this in return for a cosy game of Mah Jong on the patio (Streib 2002). The soap opera images of the old home community – the chat over the back wall, folk popping round to borrow a cup of sugar, granddad in the rocking chair, the working-class matriarch presiding over Sunday lunch – all seem to confer a fundamental sense of rightness about later life. Travelling down to Arizona in a gas-guzzling recreational vehicle with a soft-top hitched behind violates such images. As the song goes, 'there must be trouble ahead' somewhere in these balmy tourist idylls, a sense that their time and money will soon be running out, when a final retribution will ultimately lay low all the pretensions of living and enjoying life in a sunset county for ever.

Nor is this unease solely the result of a sense of injustice about the disparities of income and wealth between those who are bound to stay put and those who are free to take off. There is a deeper unease that people should choose to face the end of their lives with so little thought, and so little preparation. There seems to be a sense that such third ageism desecrates the moral identity of later life. The social construction of old age is predicated upon their being some internal cohesion within the population of retirees. It is not simply a matter of an ascribed identity, lacking in any internal authenticity. Ageing is expected to establish a common bond, a sense of connectedness with others, a common position and a set of shared interests. This view of old age implies (or wishes to see expressed) an explicitly political consciousness of ageing, and a recognition of the need to establish a common platform for seniors, pensioners, the old, the elderly, the aged or the retired. In this final section of the chapter, we address these contrasting positions: one predicated on a set of shared interests uniting those in later life, versus one that posits a neo-tribalism among retirees who seek to keep retirement away from the ascribed communities of the fourth age.

Unlike most other communities of identity, old age has not been brought into being by its own agency (Weeks 1998: 37). As we have shown, the social category of old age is primarily a category of social policy, a product of industrialization and the conflicts of class society. Attempts to articulate the interests of the old *qua* the old have always been problematic. State pensions were an outcome of a broader set of social reforms aimed at various representations of the working class, as sick, injured or disabled workers, as well as the 'dependants' of these workers – widows, mothers and children. In general, they were not the consequence of a particular set of demands by older people themselves. The specific interests of older people have been treated as benefits of social citizenship rather than issues of identity. Consequently, it is not surprising that movements of older people have failed to have the impact that their numbers suggest that they should have had. Those advocating for the interests of the old have operated within the province of charity rather than as members of a potentially 'transgressive' mass movement. The state-created category of 'pensioner' offered none of the possibilities for 'difference' that opened up to the other social identities emerging out of the cultural maelstrom of the 1960s. The idea of 'grey power', as an equal partner with black or gay power in a politics of liberation, has scarcely moved on from being wishful thinking.

Writers such as Sara Arber and Jay Ginn (1991) have pointed to the fact that movements such as feminism have often used ageism as a way of articulating their own interests by portraying the needs of older people as an oppressive burden. This lack of symmetry between the advocates for 'old age' and other social movements was demonstrated in the UK controversy over young disabled people being placed in residential settings alongside elderly patients (Campbell 2003). While older people may have common interests, their traditional position within the social structure places them in a difficult situation. They continue to be tied by their pre-modern position as the deserving poor, whose needs are best represented by charitable institutions or by their more modern status as state pensioners whose needs are articulated within the wider discourse of social policy. Neither position offers much leverage for a distinct political identity – the main option being to be proved worthy of receiving a larger slice of welfare than others.

It is not, however, a position without possibilities. As the movements based around difference have found, it is not their radicalism *vis-à-vis* the existing order that gets them noticed as communities of interest, but rather their capacity to colonize positions of social influence and command potential economic resources (Halter 2000: ch. 6). This is as true for those in later life as it is for members of the newly socially included communities of identity (Castells 1997: 54). It is also the case that such inclusion is not general; rather, it is symbolic, with as many divisions being smoothed over as being acknowledged. The attempt to replace the symbolic representation of old age as a social and moral category of need with a later-life identity typified by leisure, however, has proved less capable of securing external support.

The first attempt to politicize such an identity for old age goes back to the 1930s and the Townsendite movement. The slogan of the Townsendite movement was stark in its demands – *Youth for*

Work, Old Age for Leisure (Mitchell 2000). The movement known as Old Age Revolving Pensions Ltd sought a social wage of $200 per month for all those aged 60 and over who volunteered to leave work. The monthly pension had to be spent, not saved, and was to be funded through a sales transaction tax. Developed at the height of the Depression, the Townsendite movement grew into a national movement appealing unsurprisingly to the poor and those over 50. It influenced the framing of the 1935 Social Security Act and continued to exert a more general influence upon the iconography of later life, which treated retirement from the labour force as a social good precisely because it transformed older people from 'failing' producers into 'successful' consumers.

The link between the Townsendite movement and the American Association of Retired Persons (AARP) lies not only in both movements' orientation towards later life as consumption, but also in the suspicion that they were both 'rackets' designed to trick the old out of their money (Mitchell 2000: 95; Morris 1997). However, while the Townsendite movement petered out into a series of social clubs for retirees, the AARP has grown in stature and size, moving from its original function as an aide to the pension and insurance industries, to being a powerful advocate for America's retired population (Messinger 1955). This transformation in the role of the AARP has been achieved by maintaining a focus upon retired people as customers rather than welfare recipients, by maintaining an image of retirement as a time of opportunity, and by presenting images of older people as ideally rich, glamorous and fit.

Whether the forty million members of the AARP constitute a community of identity can be contested; but they pay their dues, receive their monthly magazine, and substantial numbers engage with the AARP's political agenda. They share a community of interest as consumers. By comparison, the Gray Panthers remain a minority organization, barely surviving the death of their leader. What is remarkable is the symbolism that has been attached by the gerontological community to this radical movement for old age, in a country not noted for the success of its radical parties. No doubt the Gray Panthers have a certain appeal to the veterans of radical social democracy, because their basic message demands 'respect' for the aged on the basis that they are rejected and despised for their 'powerlessness, wrinkled skin and physical limitations'.[7] Significantly, this places them as victims of an ageist society, rather than as individuals who have been denied opportunities to fully participate in society.

In Europe, the political representation of later life remains trapped within the politics of pensions. While it can be argued that pensions continue to be a key site of conflict for *working people*, the creation of pensioner parties adds little to this agenda. The presence of significant numbers of pensioners within Italy's trade union movement demonstrates the potential conjoining of interests between those in and out of work, but it is one that is not predicated upon an assumed communality of age (Chiarini 1999). It seems also to be the case that the retrenchment of the European welfare state has fostered the emergence of a few national pensioner parties, but these parties have difficulties in sustaining a broad unity of purpose among the retired population. They risk developing an incompatible mix of social democratic claims for improved pensions and health care alongside nationalistic attitudes towards immigration and other cultures.

Evers and Wolf (1999) have pointed out that as retired people move from a position of weakness to one of relative strength, a conflict arises between consumerist and lobbying perspectives and the pursuit of claims for inclusive citizenship and social protection (Evers and Wolf 1999: 60). In the UK context this is demonstrated by the contrast between largely middle-class interest groups and the broader representative organizations of pensioners. The former, exemplified by the Equitable Members Action Group, seek to secure their own annuities in the face of commercial difficulties, as well as improving corporate governance of investment institutions in the UK. The latter, represented by the trades union-focused UK National Pensioners Convention, campaign for higher state retirement pensions as well as better health and social care provision.

Nor does research into age and voting behaviour suggest a political focus around 'ageing' issues within the retired population. While older cohorts are more likely to vote, their voting preferences rarely demonstrate a distinct age-associated profile. In his analysis of US age-related voting behaviour, Binstock concludes that 'older voters have not shown monolithic tendencies in their electoral decision making. Their ballots tend to distribute among candidates in roughly the same patterns as do those of other age groups and the electorate as a whole. They have not proved to be important in determining the outcome of elections' (Binstock 2000: 29). This is also true for the UK (see Vincent 1999: 101). Since the realization of universal suffrage, voting preferences have shown considerable inter-generational and lifecourse stability, with a broad polarization between parties of the Left and labour and parties of the Right and property (Heath, Jowell and Curtis 1985; Lane and Ersson 1999). This polarity has begun to lose its former coherence, and voting patterns have become less predictable and less stable as the constituencies of Modernity 1 have gradually fragmented into varieties of local 'third ways' (Crouch 1999: 343). Under these circumstances one might anticipate that 'issue politics' would play a greater role in determining people's voting preferences, and that past and present links to work, home and family might become less powerful determinates of political choices. Even if 'issue' politics come to overshadow the former communities of interest representing neighbourhood and class, it seems unlikely that this will lead to the politicization of the retired as an 'age'-group. Old age may not be an adequate basis for politics. Equally, it is unlikely that 'generational' accounting will unite and activate a new politics around particular 'birth cohorts'.

Conclusion

What, then, constitutes community in the twenty first century? The solidaristic configurations of Modernity 1 are fragmenting. The weight of neighbourhood, work and family traditions has become less heavy. In a 'community-lite' world, trading bureaucratic individualism for the individualized lifestyles of the market creates increased opportunities as well as increased risks. This is as true in later life as it is earlier in life, but the risks are greater as the scope for playing the market narrows. For many, the family remains a resource and a buffer across the lifecourse even as it changes in form and function. For a small but growing minority of retired people, their path through life has given them access to sufficient material, social and human capital to allow them to benefit from the 'neo-tribalism' of the various communities of identity, place and belonging of late modernity. Arguably, those benefits derive from the foundations of a modernity that no longer exists. Those retiring at the end of the twentieth and start of the twenty-first century might seem the lucky ones, living and profiting from both modernities. Whether those whose adult lives are spent entirely within the more recent form of modernity will fare better or worse remains to be seen.

But whatever the future of later life, it seems unlikely ever again to be walled in by the old communities of 'class' or 'generational' solidarity. Ageing without boundaries may not be possible, but those boundaries are being challenged all the time. Attempts to frame these challenges in terms of an inter-generational crisis are mistaken. Most of those retiring in the early twenty-first century are beneficiaries of the generational divide that split Modernity 2 from Modernity 1. They have had both the stability as well as the benefits of mass consumer society. Within the more fluid society that has emerged in the wake of this divide, the communities of propinquity that still remain are incapable of fostering the cultural fields of the third age. Surprisingly, perhaps, families rather than communities have shown more resilience in adjusting to the new conditions of social life. Finding sufficient space for ageing outside the family remains a central challenge: what seems clear is that whatever results will have to be 'community-lite'.

8

Fog-lamps and Leitmotifs

In a special issue of the *British Journal of Sociology* on the tasks facing sociology in the new millennium, Gosta Esping-Andersen argued that the discipline lacks contemporary leitmotifs with which to grasp the turbulence associated with the disappearance of 'society as usual' (Esping-Andersen 2000). No satisfactory leitmotifs can emerge, he adds, at least not until the fog has lifted to reveal 'some kind of stable equilibrium with historical staying power, broad cross-societal diffusion and *causal impact'* (Esping-Andersen 2000: 65). He identifies three possible responses to this dilemma. The first is to abandon any hope of new structures emerging and reconcile ourselves to constantly surfing over the social landscapes of 'post-modernity'. The second is to deny that anything has really changed and continue using the classical leitmotifs of modernity. The third is to bide our time and 'purchase fog lamps . . . to illuminate more powerfully the immediate vicinity, the details just before our eyes . . . [applying] intentional and purposeful empiricism' (Esping-Andersen 2000: 72)

Similar dilemmas confront those studying ageing. It is clear that Western societies are ageing, but what is not clear is what ageing means in an ageing society. Later life seems to have become more diffuse, its parameters less easily demarcated, and its social position too contradictory to pin down. We have argued that the social nature of ageing is conditioned by the structures in which it is embroiled: namely, class, cohort and community. While ageing does not disappear in an ageing society, we cannot assume that it continues 'as usual'. Many of the concepts that have convention-ally been used to interpret the position of people in later life (e.g. as socially disengaged, as a de-commodified class, or as structurally dependent upon the institutions of the state) seem insufficient to address the changing contexts of an ageing society.

Where we break with Esping-Andersen is in his 'wait and see' approach to the development of new leitmotifs with which to interpret 'the messy present'. Rather than prepare the way for these new leitmotifs by undertaking deeper, wider and lengthier surveys and studies of 'the elderly', we believe it is *not* too early to define the leitmotif of our ageing societies. Only through elaborating new leitmotifs can we begin to integrate and make sense of the voluminous data that have already been collected about 'older' people (as well as recognizing what is present 'by its absence' from such surveys). Without such a contextual understanding, we cannot make sense of the many paradoxes that surround contemporary later life. We first attempted to develop such leitmotifs in *Cultures of Ageing*, by focusing on the effects of the cultural turn on ageing studies, drawing attention to the transformative narratives of the self, citizenship and body as they applied to ageing and later life (Gilleard and Higgs 2000). In this volume, we have contextualized this approach by further developing the concepts of Modernity 2 and 'generational field' as they might apply to later life. We have shown that many of the issues surrounding ageing societies are ones of modernity's making: namely, the rise in life expectancy, the fiscal crisis of pensions funding, the problems of urbanization and urban communities, and the changing nature of household and family. But they are also issues related to the agency of post-war cohorts. The transformation of later life from residual category to leisure culture emerged out of the rising affluence of those who rejected the view that saw utility only in labour. The reflexive habitus of post-war cohorts meant that the affluence they gained, rather than being used simply as a means of displaying wealth, served to open out new cultural possibilities which transformed not only their lives but the lives of the 'generations' that surrounded them.

Illuminating the Third Age: the Role of the Generational Field

In the introductory chapter of this book, we argued that the third age was neither a stage of life nor a state of mind, but a cultural field formed by the changing contexts that make up the social world. While many of its boundaries have been shaped, but not set, by the changing relationship between capital, labour and the state, the emergence of the third age as a cultural field has been realized most particularly within the lifecourse of 'axial' birth cohorts. Its appearance as a distinct cultural space has also been predicated upon the decline of the 'old' communities of propinquity. Consequently, we have used the classical categories of class, generation and community to illuminate the third age. In doing so, we have constructed an interpretative structure for later life that emphasizes its distinctiveness. As with any ideal type, much of our analysis exaggerates and abstracts particular patterns and configurations of the social world. It would be absurd to assume that adults of a particular age-group can be represented collectively as third agers, just as it would be senseless to assume that the third age is a form of cultural capital that is the property of a single class, cohort or community.

We have represented the third age as a generational field whose origins lie in the 'youth culture' of the 1950s and 1960s. Participants in post-war youth culture acquired habitus, to pursue our sequestration of Bourdieu's terminology, which have evolved and multiplied during the course of their lifetimes, affecting the lifestyles of cohorts born before and after these war babies. Central to those habitus have been new styles and new approaches to consumption arising from the epigenesis of mass culture (Kammen 1999: 179). What was novel about this new form of consumption was its capacity to generate 'lifestyles' that were fashioned differently from the 'styles of life' that were traditionally associated with particular classes occupying specific cultural niches in modern society. Consciousness of this transition and its underlying 'entelechy' was most often expressed by members of the 'radical' middle classes whose age placed them 'above' and 'to one side' of the real site of transition.[1] It was this group who spoke of youth's desire to break away from a society where 'you knew who people were from the way they spoke, you knew where they came from, the way they dressed, you knew what sort of jobs'.[2] Exemplified in the early disenchantment of Jimmy Porter in *Look Back in Anger* and Holden Caulfield in *Catcher in the Rye*, the mood of protest and rebellion reverberated in the youth of the time. This mood

traversed many of the distinctions of class and crossed the boundaries of national communities. But its true significance was not just
in the emergence of a youth culture, important though that was,
but its emergence within a growing mass culture that was capable
of being extended to, expressed and acted upon at every stage of
life. Socialization into the new lifestyles of consumption permeated the lives not just of the participants in post-war 'youth
culture, but of all those who have grown up since the watershed
era of the 1960s.

The cultural space of the third age continues to be underpinned
by the capacity to spend. As with its origins, so now as it is
expressed in the lifestyles of 'modern maturity', this is not the
'conspicuous consumption' of Modernity 1 that was described by
Veblen (1953). Rather, it is consumption arising from the aspirations of agency. The desire for freedom was keenly felt by the post-
war youth of America and Europe. Consumption became the site
where those aspirations were most readily met. The expression
of those aspirations through consumption formed the lifestyle
habitus that now define the third age. Two conditions were necessary for its emergence: first, an expansion in the number of
people with discretionary spending power, and second, the creation of new sites of consumption, disembedded from the communal settings of the past. As 'self-service' became the dominant
form of consumption – exemplified in the new supermarkets,
fashion boutiques, record shops and new-style department stores
– individualization and differentiation became key. Mass culture
involved the rejection of older forms of popular culture, replacing them with increasingly segmented, cross-cutting lifestyles that
maintained difference from the past along with distinction in the
present.

As one commentator of the time argued, the 1950s and 1960s
were as much a 'neophiliac' as a 'youth-oriented' culture (Booker
1970). A desire for what was 'now', what was new and different,
was valued in and of itself. This was not so much as in earlier
modernity because the new was a synonym for progress, but
because it served to distance this 'new' generation from the 'old'
one. The desire to embrace what was new and reject what was old
was felt at least as strongly by working-class youth as it was by
the middle class. It focused upon sources of *horizontal* differen-

tiation, eliding 'youth' with 'freedom' and 'leisure'. In that sense, the origins of the third age lie in a cultural field which early on defined itself as resistance to the constrictions and limitations of 'old' ways and 'old' styles of living. Past habits of consumption constrain future opportunities. Those who grew up spending freely earlier in life are more likely to continue to spend freely later in life (see Roberts 2004). In the generational field of Modernity 1, consumption as a site of agency was quite restricted, particularly for the majority of the working-class population.[3] The differentiation that could be achieved within classes was considerably less than that between classes. Hence class-based cultures and class-based styles of life formed the dominant sources of social differentiation. Further differentiation was restricted by the limited availability of goods and services, the constraints imposed by existing moral communities of taste, and the limited existence of discretionary spending. In the first decades of the twentieth century, food alone consumed over half of all the costs of living for the working classes with 95 per cent of family expenditure devoted to purchasing the necessities of food, housing, fuel and clothing.[4] By contrast, in the early twenty-first century, 18 per cent of household expenditure is used to purchase 'leisure goods and services', while food accounts for only 16 per cent.[5] The post war expansion in discretionary spending across much of the general population, and its subsequent extension over much of the life-course, has offered more people than ever access to the agency of 'lifestyle choices'. Individual differentiation has become the dominant aspect of Modernity 2.

So, the third age is a field constituted by agency. It represents the freedom to choose and the freedom to spend time and money in pursuit of individual lifestyle goals.[6] Though we refer to these goals as 'individualized', the choices that are made by individuals may well be neither 'selfish', 'self-serving', nor 'destructive of social capital'. For example, significant inter-generational transfers of resources continue to be made from older to younger generations (see Bawin-Legros and Stassen 2002; Kohli 1999). Retirees leaving behind their old local communities are actively creating new communities of propinquity which bring in their wake not only new opportunities for retirees themselves but significant material benefits for the 'receiving' communities (Walters 2002).

Those participating in the third age add human capital to society in many other ways, whether through active volunteering, acting as grandparents, or through the more passive role of maintaining a social presence in residential areas that would otherwise be deserted during the hours of the working day. As a cultural field, the third age presents opportunities for lifestyle choices that are not devalued by the too ready attributions of 'agedness'. Providing the opportunity to live longer whilst not becoming old, the third age adds value to a longer life (A. E. Barrett 2003). Though the third age cannot be exemplified in the particularities of any individual life, individual lives possess potential iconic value in illustrating the ideals and rehearsing the ideologies of actively living the third age – to which the cover stories of *Modern Maturity* and *AARP The Magazine* continue to bear witness.

Illuminating the Third Age: Its Economic Base

We would scarcely be 'illuminating' the third age by privileging its status as a site of agency without giving due weight to its economic underpinning. The third age has come about because of mass affluence, the result of increased productivity, expanding markets and rising real incomes. Between 1950 and 2000, average annual growth in household incomes exceeded 3 per cent in most OECD countries (OECD 2001b). While that growth has not been universal or constant over individual lifecourses, it has had a general cumulative beneficial effect that has been translated into higher living standards for most people now aged 60 and over. These benefits have become more evident in recent decades. They are the product of three processes: increases in social transfers arising from contributory social insurance schemes, increases in the coverage and benefits of personal and occupational pensions, and wider ownership of capital assets, notably home ownership and to a lesser extent personal investments and inter-generational transfers. The material connection between working life and post-working life provides the explanation both for rising standards of living in later life, as well as increasing sources of differentiation in later life, and for the consequent variation in the opportunities for discretionary spending in retirement.

Class and the nature of modern capitalism have undergone many changes during the lifetime of those who have grown up during the second half of the twentieth century. Stable blue-collar jobs and white-collar careers are no longer the dominant styles of work in the industrialized world. Because those who formally own capital are a more diffuse, numerous and variegated group than they were in the early days of industrial capitalism, they are generally less able to exercise effective power. At the same time, those who control the destinations and flows of capital have gained considerably in power. In consequence, there has been a shift of emphasis away from maximizing the productivity of labour to maximizing the rate of return on capital. Stock options have transformed the position of the CEO, creating new sites of conflict between workers, shareholders, directors and trust fund managers, over which the state has limited powers of influence. The growing reality of international financial regulations and principles, often entered into by nation-states in order to gain access to funds, goes beyond governance to provide the rules for government. On the other side, it has been claimed that governments' ability and willingness to participate in such international agreements deregulating the global economy is itself predicated upon the existence of stable systems of social protection. Any significant risks to national incomes arising from changes in global arrangements are just as likely to lead to a withdrawal from those arrangements, as they are to cutbacks in social protection (Rieger and Liebfried 2003). Others have argued that 'retrenchment' in national systems of social protection is made difficult in any case because of the massive expansion of welfare as a source of secure employment and local political power. This new debate between markets and states is no longer solely encompassed by national struggles between capital and labour. The conflicts arising from the management of national programmes of social protection welfare in Modernity 2 take place on sites that are quite different from the sites where welfare provision struggled to grow. While the latter focused upon issues of social class, modernization and democratization, the former now centre upon political institutions, party systems and policy discourse (Green-Pedersen and Haverland 2002).

Within these new contexts, pensions have moved to occupy a central position in shaping the nature of global capital flows and patterns of investment. This has had an obvious direct impact upon the distribution of income and wealth across the lifecourse. The indirect role of global capital markets on social policy has meant that the third age is a cultural field whose boundaries are no longer controlled simply by the actions of governing national elites whose decisions about the appropriate roles of 'the elderly' are determinate. Not only is there growing privatization of retirement income across a growing range of countries, but the growing facility of shifting capital within the global economy means that for a significant minority, retirement need no longer be confined to national boundaries (Ackers and Dwyer 2004). This movement in the balance between the nation-state and the market is played out in different ways in different national economies, but the role of the market shows little sign of yielding to the social policy imperatives of 'ageing' nation-states.

Illuminating the Third Age: Leaving Old Age Behind?

Ageing societies do not make the individual experience of age disappear, but the question is why they seem unable to 'normalize' it. Now that being 60 is as common as being 16, the lack of any consensus over the social meaning of ageing is perhaps not quite so surprising. If we reflect upon the time it took to establish a status for the teenager after the institutions of universal secondary education were put in place, then one might also expect that after the institution of universal retirement, retired people might have achieved a clearer place within our society. As already intimated, a growing factor in the failure to establish any fixed form for the third age is the instability in the relationship between the state and the market. The third age is a cultural field that has become less contingent on particular state welfare policies. But other factors are also at work. The organization of everyday life has been transformed. The social space of home, work and 'play' is less bounded. Individual homes have become cultural locations of increasing importance to people of all ages, overshadowing other sites of productive and leisured activity. This is particularly so when homes are compared to other 'social' places marking out a local community, such as pubs, cafés, shops and public amenities.

Lone adults of different ages and backgrounds contribute to the definition of the domestic space of home as much as multigenerational families do. Retired people typically live alone or with one other retired person, but their aloneness is no longer the necessary consequence of neglect, poverty and stigmatization. Increasingly, they share a set of similar domestic circumstances with a wide, if scarcely imagined, community of younger couples and single people. Each conducts his or her own life in a more intensely private manner than before. When there is no one around to define the tragedy of retirement, its tragic nature dissolves. To be alone and outside the labour market is no longer to be old. Old age is a status conferred by others, one that is progressively restricted to the ascribed communities of the fourth age. For the majority, what continues is the symbolic connectedness of individualized lives.

The demise of the local community and its kinship networks is by no means total. But it is, more and more, a historical form of modern life. Those left behind to define and sustain it risk becoming 'old' in consequence. The rise of virtual or symbolic communities has enabled various status groups to acquire new forms of social capital. Whilst making use of the virtual community that telecommunications technology has created, a symbolic community of 'senior citizens' has proved more difficult to realize. Members of 'visible' and 'invisible' minorities have achieved a place within society through such symbolic communities, which, however contested, offer potential access to power, influence and a degree of respect. Later life does not seem likely to become such a site. Ageing seems too common and too diffuse to provide the clear symbolic identity that social movements seem to require. To amplify this point, it is useful to consider the multiple issues and interests that might compete as appropriate signifiers for such a symbolic communal identity.

Should people unite and form a community of interest around pensions? If so, what sort of pensioners should they be? Campaigners for higher state pensions? Victims or losers from mismanaged private pension schemes? Should they coalesce around their status as retirees? Again what kind of retirees should they be? Discarded workers, small-scale rentiers, pioneers of postworking lifestyles, or the unruly members of a reserve army of labour? Alternatively, should they centre their common interests on health? However, what sort of patients' union should they form? One of commodified customers, assertive clients, or marginalized patients further subdivided into the holistically geriatric and the medicalized particular? The multiplicity of positions, as well as the competing claims for a social foundation for later life, suggest that membership of a symbolic community will appeal only to those older people who can be defined by a distinction beyond that of work (such as race or sexual orientation). A broad coalition of 'the aged' seems improbable.

The demise of community, rather than undermining the conditions for a later lifestyle, can be thought of as creating opportunities for the social and cultural expansion of post-working lifestyles. Age is more important to people in contemporary society than ever before. Without knowledge of our date of birth we can scarcely exercise citizenship or function as consumers. But consciousness of age and ageing does not begin or end at any one birthday. Coping with ill health and coping with wrinkles are personal tasks, for which there is no shortage of collective solutions. Rather than seek solidarity by placing the boundaries of chronological age around the third age, it can be argued that it is precisely through its multiple positionalities and its ability to escape being bound to one gender, one class or one age-group that the third age can best flourish.

What Lies Beyond: the Darker Side of the Third Age

And what of those who cannot play these 'post-modern games'? There are many retired people whose participation in the third age is minimal, and a minority for whom the idea of a third age cannot be envisaged. Are the contexts that are fostering diversity in later life, *in reality*, reflecting and even increasing the divisions of inequality in old age? Is there a darker side to the third age that our notional fog-lamps fail to show up? Two broad critiques of our position are commonly made. The first, coming from the 'political economy' approach, emphasizes the material inequalities that support the third age, while the second, which is more philosophically oriented, focuses upon the problems raised by the non-normative, unnatural 'agelessness' that seems to be privileged by the third age.

Taking the 'economistic' critique first, three types of evidence are used to argue that diversity maps directly on to inequality in later life. The 'emergence' of the third age is seen as the consequence of economic inequality among the retired populations of Western society (e.g. Arber and Ginn 1995: 176; Phillipson 1998: 81–3). Correlations between low income, limited social capital, poor health and limited participation in 'leisure' suggest a common underlying process (Bury 1995). Many argue that the freedom not to accept a definition of oneself as 'old' or 'elderly' and to continue to live 'successfully' outside the ascribed communities of the fourth age (i.e. not attending 'old age' day centres or 'geriatric' day hospitals, not having to spend respite 'vacations' in residential or nursing homes, and so on) requires a particular combination of material, social and cultural 'capital' (Collins, Estes and Bradshaw 2001: 162–3).

Perhaps the first point to be made is that participants in a cultural field do not define that field. Income and expenditure are closely linked. The fact that different birth cohorts differentially own, and hence make differential use of, material technology such as mobile phones, personal computers and CD players that enable a 'generational' culture to be expressed suggests that a distinction between 'economic' and 'generational' position needs to be made. In 2001, two out of three British women aged 60 and over owned a mobile (cell) phone. This was true for most socio-economic groups. Mobile phone ownership amongst women aged 75 and over was less than half that, and even amongst those from the highest socio-economic grouping only a third (34 per cent) owned one. Socio-economic differentials in mobile phone ownership amongst younger cohorts are quite minimal: 91 per cent of women from professional and managerial backgrounds own one, as do 84 per cent of women from unskilled backgrounds.[7] A similar point could be made about colour TVs in the 1970s, or about VCRs in the 1980s (Longhurst and Savage 1996). Socio-economic differences tend to be very evident during the early sale and distribution of these leisure goods, but they rapidly decline. This decline is more rapid in younger cohorts, where product differentiation replaces take-up. But in recent times, there has been a rapid spread upward and outward across older generations, though the oldest old are still often excluded.

Utilizing Bourdieu's more general discussion of cultural distinction, many activities associated with the third age demonstrate patterns of variation that are not 'a direct product of economic necessity' (Bourdieu 1992: 178). In Britain, entrance to most museums is free, but there are still large variations in patterns of visiting them, which closely mirror variations in educational background (see Bagnell 1996). Likewise in the USA, where the core arts receive only limited levels of public financial support, rates of attendance at jazz, opera and ballet by those aged 55–74 has increased remarkably over recent years in ways that cannot be explained by reference to growing wealth or education.[8]

We would reiterate that the sources of inequality in the twenty-first century no longer map *simply* on to the old binary divisions of class. This is so across much of the lifecourse. While the oldest birth cohorts retain many of those material, social and cultural divisions, those now exiting the labour market are less easily positioned by the binary opposition of 'working' versus 'middle' class. Temporal vicissitudes in the post-war economy have resulted in increasingly variable membership of the new leisure class. Those who joined a nationalized industry with a defined benefits occupational pension scheme and who are seeing it through to retirement will experience a very different outcome in later life from those who took the opportunity in the 1980s to 'switch' to a private pension that has since under-performed. Middle managers of enterprises such as Enron face a potentially very different future in later life from middle managers who joined Microsoft. American employees earning similar wages who took up their firms' occupational pension plan can still experience very different outcomes, depending on whether their employer has stayed with or switched away from a defined benefits (DB) scheme. Equally, there are also winners and losers in direct contribution (DC) schemes, depending upon the particular investment packages that fund managers have put together (Ghilarducci 1992).

In a society of 'second chances', where nothing can be planned to successful completion, what matters is whether and how one engages with the habitus of choice (Giddens 1991: 82–7). In the context of Modernity 2, luck has to play some role. In the 1960s and 1970s, very few could have anticipated the housing boom of the late twentieth century. Equally, hardly anyone could have anticipated that the New York Stock Exchange index would break the 10,000 mark in the 1990s. Whether or not pension fund members actually benefited from this boom has been a matter of luck and the operations of a 'disorganized capitalism'. The French worker who only a few years before was happily contemplating a secure, early retirement from the private sector now finds his or her hopes dashed by the pension reforms that were instituted in the 1990s.

Despite the salience of freedom of choice in the lives of post-war cohorts, retirement has proved resistant to being incorporated into the habitus of personalized finance and consumer choice. Study after study has shown that the majority of people in both the United States and Europe have little idea of their likely income in retirement; nor do they seem aware of how it is organized (Chan and Stevens 2003). The dark side of the third age cannot be denied. It owes its origins to a society of second chances. Engagement with personal choice and individual risk that was such a hallmark of the generational field of which the third age is a part has, as the other side of the coin, the problem of individual failure. Failure to choose is as much a failure of choice as making the wrong choice (Bauman 2001: 46–7). Even making the 'right' choice is no guarantee of final success. The openness of Modernity 2 ensures that this can never be the case. The third age cannot escape its indeterminacy. As state policies attempt to shift responsibility for income replacement after retirement toward the individual, the resulting risk and uncertainty this poses then problematize the agency that this generation once celebrated in its collectively voiced wish to 'be free'.[9]

Grey Spectres, Global Shadows

Just as the 'progressive liberation of capital from labour'[10] has added new and different sources of inequality to society, so the liberation of 'ageing' from 'old age' is creating new dilemmas of justice which question the principle of just desserts. The moral critique of the third age focuses upon its putative false consciousness. The promotion of the third age as a cultural field dominated by the indeterminacies of consumption and grounded upon the openness of human desire is seen as the working of a sinister and seductive market, a market that insidiously undermines the moral community from which alone individuals can confront the limitations of the body and the finality of life. By outlining and advancing the cultural boundaries of the third age, the argument goes, a fourth age is deliberately and systematically emptied of all meaning beyond that of social and personal waste. As one commentator writes, 'whereas policy has been a major contributing factor behind the creation of the third age, it has been, virtually everywhere, inadequate or misdirected in addressing the problems of the fourth age' (Hudson 1999: 334).

What opportunities exist for individuals and their families to make sense of the erosion of memory and identity that is senility? How are the weaknesses of the body rendered tolerable to the once proud owners of bodies fit for a purpose? How should individuals make sense of the slow decline of their bodily organs when death, not age, advances? By making the functional limitations of the body the signs of a failed identity, the third age enriches its own 'field' at the cost of impoverishing old age. Such critics argue that the shadows of mortality cannot be so easily removed by the scalpel or the endless application of hair colourants. Equally, the personal collapse into physical dependency will not goad the global market into funding a rescue package for the fourth age.

No doubt old age does not form part of the shopping trolley of consumer society; but waving the 'grim reaper' in front of the clients of aesthetic surgery clinics is unlikely to cause them to eschew prospects for a smoother face or a firmer figure. That life is finite is more widely acknowledged now than in the past, when the miseries of everyday existence called for religious sources of comfort. The third age is not fashioned by its denial of finitude. Indeed, it is a part of a secular socialization that has brought about the confrontation with human finitude. Dementia is not made more comfortable, nor emphysema more admirable, by retired people foregoing the gym, kicking off their trainers, deserting cruise ships, or abstaining from playing the 'slots' in Las Vegas.

But, it is argued, older and poorer patients end up being less well tended because the resources of the third age remain locked in cycles of cumulative personal and intra-familial advantage rather than being progressively redistributed to reduce poverty and improve health care. These resources are retained, through regressive pension policies, in the hands of those who largely do not have to care. Declining support for collective risk sharing, the substitution of consumer choice for political choice, and the growing emphasis upon private solutions to public ills are all no doubt elements shaping the generational field of which 'third ageism' forms a part. But if making more of life as a third age project makes less of it as a fourth age one, this hardly seems unjust or unfair. The political and social structures that have brought this about are not mainly of their doing. Inequality and unfairness are constant features of the different forms of modernity. The fact that the third age is not dominated by a frugal lifestyle devoted to 'precautionary after-care' or filled with endless hours of selfless volunteering may be a source of chagrin to some, but as one article has pointed out with regard to older Minnesotan gamblers, 'You bet they're having fun!' (Hope and Havir 2002).

Global Governance and the Limits of Later Life

More significant than the criticisms developed by either the political or the moral economy approaches is the argument that the true constraints on the development of the third age lie in the encroachments of global capitalism. The capacity of the state to secure the conditions for an 'enriched' later life is becoming more limited.[11] The conflict of interest between global capital and nation-states has been a constant feature of the modern world (Harris 2003). The dominant political models of the nineteenth century placed economic advance at the heart of ruling strategies. These were gradually superseded in the twentieth century by the need for social welfare in cementing the nation-state. The contradictions between national welfare and capital accumulation seemed capable of being contained in the decades immediately following the Second World War. After the oil crisis, the instability of this trade-off became apparent. Global financial institutions such as the IMF and the World Bank sought to restructure the world according to their model. Central to this was the reduction of social expenditure and a focus upon national competitiveness.[12] Ruling elites saw their fortunes measured by the international value of their free-floating currencies and the extent to which they could draw in foreign investment. The decoupling of the economic system and the nation-state after the 'big bang' removed many of the constraints on the global trading of what were once nationally based stocks, shares and currencies (Hirst and Thompson 1999: 48–61). The idea of management and markets which flowed from this turned what was previously public expenditure into just another sector of the economy, whose performance was to be judged according to the same criteria as were applied to all who control capital.

The nation-state seems to have acquired the role of an administrative structure 'concerned with the conduct of conduct' (Thrift 2000: 71), dealing primarily with those parts of the economy that are either problematic or cannot be relocated or which need subsidies in order to meet the social goals. A key problem, then, is how to define these social goals and how best to subsidize them. This conflict affects international as well as national communities. The constraints placed on the nation-state by global markets, as well as the commodification of citizens as consumers rather than producers, make it harder to determine collective social outcomes. Later life is no longer simply the outcome of a social compact. The financial, social and cultural fabric supporting later life is woven (in part) out of systems of global capital and global governance that make all such national compacts contingent. Even if, as critics of globalization have maintained, this represents not so much an end-point 'as a tendency to which there are counter-tendencies' (Hay and Marsh 2000: 6), it seems unlikely that sufficient communality of interests now exists amongst either the retired or the working populations of Western nation-states to attempt a clear and coherent counter-movement capable of reviving *les trentes glorieuses*. Rather, responses are likely to continue to be partial, fragmented and 'reflexive', much in the way that the American Association of Retired Persons (AARP) has responded to the recent revisions in Medicare provision in the USA.[13]

Who, then, controls the third age? Like all choices, consumer choice does not take place in circumstances of everyone's choosing. Those making the choices can foresee few of the consequences of choices that are made over a lifetime; nor, equally, can those who seem to control the choices that can be made. The opportunities to consume, to choose, and to be free to do so will always be constrained. There will always be limits, limits arising from both the nature of social organization as well as from factors that cannot be incorporated into the organization of the social such as the pathological. There is no easy answer to Lenin's hypothetical question 'who – whom?' The third age is a site of contradictions and contestations: between the interests of nation-states and those of global markets; between the interests of those in positions of ownership of capital and those in positions of control; between those more or less advantaged members of more or less advantaged birth cohorts; and between the individualizing experience of ageing and the collective responses to it. The majority of people do not consciously plan or envision participation in a third age. The third age has emerged nevertheless. It was not planned by the state or manufactured by the market. It is not simply the cultural product of a particular set of structures operating at a particular time in a particular place. Equally, it is not just the outcome of the active choices of a particular few. In some ways it is all of these, yet none of them.

Though we cannot provide a final answer to the question of who owns the third age, what seems clear is that war babies, baby boomers and members of all subsequent twentieth-century birth cohorts have a growing stake in it. Rhetoric to the contrary notwithstanding, continuing inter-generational transfers will ensure that this will prove an inheritance that cannot quickly be spent, or one that can be easily overthrown by either the 'logic' of capital or the 'forces' of nature (Wahl 2003). The third age is a malleable field, fashioned by succeeding generations entering later life, each doing so in their own image. Modernity 2 is different from the classical phase of modernity in its transformation of the determinacies of class, cohort and community. As these co-ordinates have become less easily mapped, life's indeterminacy has grown more apparent. We have focused on these classical structures to understand the origins of the cultural field of the third age. While it seems unlikely that these leitmotifs will ever prove irrelevant in explaining its future, reducing later life to this triad only results in a blinkered and distorted view of the social terrain of later life. But without them, we are in danger of losing any sense of position from which the future can be charted.

Notes

Chapter 1   Introduction

1 There have been extensive debates on theories of patriarchy and their links with the study of class (Crompton 1996). Other approaches have focused on race/ethnicity as a key ordering principle (Smaje 2000; Spivak 1999). Such approaches, however, are not pivotal to understanding and interpreting *change* in the nature of later life.

2 It seems that such opportunities may have been more easily realized in the USA than in Europe – see Gratton (1996).

3 A 1953 survey of UK household expenditure excluded pensioner households when calculating a cost of living index because of their limited finances (single pensioner households spending less than a quarter of the average 'index' household: Ministry of Labour and National Service 1957: 244–7); a decade later Marsh still placed 'pensioners' in the lowest social class grouping ('those at the lowest level of subsistence') of 1960s Britain (Marsh 1965: 206).

4 Statistics Canada 2003.

5 Data from the US Bureau of Labor 2001: table 3.

6 Calculations are based upon the Living in Britain/General Household Survey data, treating as pensioner households those with either a single person aged over 60 or a couple, one of whom is over 60 (OPCS, 1978; 1982; 1987; 1992; 1997, respectively and ONS, 2002b), supplemented by the authors' own calculations from the 2001 Living in Britain/General Household Survey data archive, University of Essex.

7 Based upon Inland Revenue 2003: table T13.2 – Identified personal wealth in the UK, 2000, male and female – and adjusted for their estimates of population coverage within age bands. <www.inland revenue.gov.uk/stats/personal_wealth/dopw_t02_1mf.htm>, accessed 26 Oct. 2003 (Inland Revenue 2003).

8 By 1998, the highest median US family net worth could be found amongst those aged 65–74 years old (though previously, the highest net worth had been reported for those on the 'threshold' of retirement – ages 55–64) US Census Bureau 2003d: p. 445, table no. 677.

9 Figures for contemporary rates of education are derived from Vlasblom and Nekkers 2001: table 3.3.

10 For example, Myles writes: 'modern "retirement", an extended period of labour force exit driven by wealth, not by disability, is new for most people. This change was the result of rising affluence, on the one hand, and, on the other, the post war pension "revolution" that expanded access to this new wealth, however unevenly, to the majority of households. The question then is not whether we survive "population ageing" (we will). Rather, in face of an expanding acceleration of population ageing, the big questions concern whether and in what form modern retirement will survive, at what cost, and to whom? Of particular concern is whether the fiscal pressures (i.e. on the public budget) that result from population ageing will erode the democratic gains in equalising access to retirement achieved during the post war era of pension reform' (Myles 2002: 170).

Chapter 2   Class, Modernity and the Lifecourse

1 Esping-Andersen defines de-commodification as emancipation from market dependency, which he claims varies empirically according to (1) the conditions determining access to benefits, (2) the level of equivalence between market and social wages, and (3) the extensiveness of entitlements (Esping-Andersen 1990: 47).

2 These effects are not confined to relations between capital and labour, but also influence the very nature of capitalism itself. The well-established separation between ownership and control of the firm has been made more abstract by the steady expansion of the financial sector. Investment institutions have created increasingly reified forms of ownership of capital. These reach their most distant form in the trade of entirely synthetic forms of share ownership such as 'derivatives' (see Scholte 2002).

3 'What matters is that there is a general enrichment of the concrete substance of civilised life, a general reduction of risk and insecurity, an equalisation between the more and the less fortunate at all levels – between the healthy and the sick, between the employed and the unemployed, the old and the active, the bachelor and the father of a large family. Equalisation is not so much between classes as

between individuals within a population, which is now treated for this purpose, as though it were one class. Equality of status is more important than equality of income' (Marshall 1992: 33).

Chapter 3   The Nature of Class in Later Life

1 See Carter and Sutch 1996 and Lee 2002, 2003; for Europe see Woollard 2002.
2 Union veterans received a pension that was much more comprehensive (90 per cent) and more generous ($189 per year in 1910) than that offered to Confederate veterans. Only 30 per cent of ex-Confederate soldiers received a state pension, and the average value amounted to a mere $47 per year (Costa 1998: 49; Skocpol 1995). The Union pension represented about 30 per cent of an unskilled labourer's annual wage (Mitchell 2000: 16).
3 We have appropriated this term from Mannheim's idea of the relatively classless stratum of the intelligentsia. See Mannheim 1960: 137–8.
4 In this context we are restricting our use of the term 'globalization' to the internationalization of finance. We recognize that there are many other dimensions of globalization impacting upon later life (see e.g. Phillipson and Ahmed 2004).
5 For a fuller elaboration of the debates around the impact of globalization on the post-war welfare state, see Scharpf 2000; Huber and Stephens 2001; Swank 2002.

Chapter 4   Cohort and Generation and the Study of Social Change

1 For Bourdieu's elaboration of these terms, see Bourdieu and Wacquant 1996: 94–140; Bourdieu 1977: 72–95; and Wacquant 1989: 37–41.

Chapter 5   Later Life and the Two Generational Fields of Modernity

1 In Britain, from 1900 to at least 1940, 'the male working class continued to be recruited almost exclusively from manual ranks . . . [and during this period] class divisions became increasingly fixed and

certain' (Savage and Miles 1994: 40). In France, a similar situation obtained. 'Social flexibility . . . was closed down over time. For manual workers the hopes of upward mobility diminished markedly and the working class became more homogeneous' (Pinol 1993: 133).

2 In his analysis of social mobility between three generations of men during the first half of the twentieth century, Mukherjee described the stability of social class across the generations. In each generation, he concluded 'that there is a strong tendency among members of the society to cluster around the parental status' (Mukherjee 1952: 284), and that while there is a small group of 'unstable elements [*sic*]', they 'comprise only a small proportion of the total members of the society' (Mukherjee 1952: 286).

3 'Britain entered the Great War already possessing a system of free compulsory education up to the age of twelve or fourteen . . . [when] almost three quarters of children . . . were being educated in the elementary schools they had entered at the age of five [and] only a small minority of children . . . received "advance instruction" in . . . Secondary Schools' (Stevenson 1984: 248–9). The situation hardly changed until the 1944 Butler Education Act. By 1938, the proportion of children going to secondary school was still less than 15 per cent and less than 10 per cent of those starting work did so aged 16 or more (Stevenson 1984: 256–7).

4 When Mark Abrams (1951) began conducting his studies of class and consumption, he classified old age pensioners and the unemployed at the bottom rung of the ladder.

5 Between 1880 and 1950, the majority of older women who could do so lived with their children, and only a small minority lived alone in a pensioner household (Ruggles 2003). In a survey of UK household expenditure conducted in 1953, most 'pensioners' (62 per cent) did not live in pensioner households (Ministry of Labour and National Service 1957: 242–6).

6 Townsend observed that between one-half and three-quarters of all pensioners lived 'as householders with their children or lodgers or . . . as guests of their children' (Townsend 1963: 34).

7 While it is true that there was considerable household mobility during this time, reflecting the overwhelming pattern of private rental tenancies within the urban population, mobility from one town or locality to another was much less common (Benson 1989: 126–9).

8 Between 1901 and 1951, the size of the middle class grew very slowly. 'The proportion of men . . . engaged in clerical, professional

and other middle class occupations . . . increased moderately from 1881 to 1911, and has since remained nearly stationary' (Bewley 1937: p. xvi.). Between 1911 and 1959, the proportion of the workforce employed in professional, managerial or administrative positions rose from 16 per cent to 17 per cent; those in clerical positions increased from 9 per cent to 11 per cent over the same time period (Routh 1965: 145).

9 In 1918, 'only reading newspapers or socialising with family or friends occupied more spare time than movie-going for most workers' (Rosenzweig 1983: 192).

10 According to Cross, a national Gallup poll in 1938 found that 88 per cent of Americans believed they were in the middle class (Cross 2000: 75).

11 The existence of this proto 'youth culture' in the 1920s can be demonstrated by the number of films made in the 1920s that contained the words 'youth' or 'youthful' (see Hine 2000: 178–9).

12 Central to this process was the television industry, the 'giant pump fueling the machine of consumer demand, stepping up the flow of goods and services to keep living standards high and the economy expanding' (ABC Vice-President Donald Coyle, as cited in the introductory chapter of Spigel and Curtin 1997: 3).

13 According to Michael Kammen, the word 'lifestyle' was first introduced into the US dictionary in 1961, gradually replacing terms such as tastes and way of life, and 'conveying nuances of indeterminate class characteristics . . . as direct correlations between social class and lifestyle became progressively more elusive' (Kammen 1999: 243).

14 In a slightly different formulation, Christopher Lasch wrote of the 'culture of narcissism' that had been founded by the youth culture of the Sixties; a culture that, in his view, fostered 'the denial' and 'dread of age' that 'originates not in a cult of youth but in a cult of the self' (Lasch 1980: 217).

15 In Britain, Peter Townsend reported that a third of the 'old people' he interviewed had incomes below the state poverty line, while 'as many as seventy five percent . . . had an income low enough to qualify for assistance' (Townsend 1963).

16 An international opinion poll conducted in 1958 reported that 87 per cent of French people, 76 per cent of Italians, 71 per cent of British people and 64 per cent of Dutch respondents considered their countries' old age benefits 'too low', and less than 1 per cent thought them 'too high' (see W. J. Cohen 1958: 94).

17 One commentator has written: 'Those who live on their pensions alone can rarely afford to eat meat or new clothes or proper heating

or any kind of entertainment . . . [while others] eke out an existence on their own, often obliged to keep on part time jobs well beyond sixty five or seventy' (Ardagh 1970: 430).

18 More and more, the pub, bar or café frequented by men from the working classes was rejected for the dance hall, the youth club and the coffee bar. This was noted at the time by Richard Hoggart in his 1958 book, *Uses of Literacy*, in which he criticized the rising dominance of coffee bars and milk bars in the lives of working-class youth, with their seeming addiction to the relentless rock-and-roll music of the juke box. As Hill has pointed out, Hoggart saw 'the sturdy and . . . self-generated working class culture of his boyhood under threat from an imported commercial mass culture whose nature was summed up in his characteristic phrase 'candy floss world' – lacking any substance, sugary and above all, American in origin' (Hill 2002: 118–19).

Chapter 6   Community and the Nature of Belonging

1 Park's (1952) own work illustrates this dual perspective – on the one hand, describing the urban community as a source of 'moral order' (p. 177), seeing immigrant communities as adding value to the city because of their ability to bring the solidaristic self-help values of the 'village tradition' into the wider urban society (p. 71), and on the other hand, writing that 'our cities are full of junk, much of it human, i.e. men and women who have been scrapped by the industrial organization of which they were once a part' (p. 60).

2 The death of community studies was widely debated in the 1960s (e.g. Glass 1966; Stein 1964; Bell and Newby 1971). Its rebirth has been periodically proclaimed ever since (e.g. Bulmer 1985; Crow 2000). The emergence of systematic national household surveys conducted since the 1960s has done much to ensure that empirical research into 'local communities' has a more limited effect than it once did, when, in the first half of the twentieth century, they came to serve as a proxy for a more general investigation into 'the state of society'.

3 In the mid-Fifties, 40 per cent of British homes had a TV, 20 per cent a washing machine, and 10 per cent a fridge and a telephone; by the mid-Sixties, 88 per cent had a TV, 60 per cent a washing machine, 45 per cent a fridge, and 40 per cent a telephone (Millar 1966: 205).

4 For an earlier recognition of the desire amongst young Americans for 'a style of life that was *sui generis*, rather than a place fixed in a geo-

graphically particularised community', see Dwight Macdonald's article 'A caste, a culture, a market', which appeared in the November 1958 issue of *The New Yorker*.

Chapter 7 Community in Later Life

1 The term is derived from Talcott Parsons, and is cited by Beck-Gernsheim (2002: p. ix).
2 By this, we mean the communitarian crisis, articulated in various ways by writers such as Etzioni (1996), Fukuyama (1996), Gray (1997) and Putnam (2001).
3 There is an extensive literature demonstrating the inverse relationship between adult age and residential migration (see Rogers 1988). This, of course, tells us very little about the desires of those who stay and those who move.
4 The extent of 'ageing in place' of older people in working-class Britain is evident in the recent study by Chris Phillipson and his colleagues (Phillipson et al. 1999). Contemporary evidence shows that the poorer an older person (or couple) is, the more likely it is that they will be living with their children. This appears to be a significant reversal of the situation of much of the last 150 years, when the poor could not afford to take in their ageing parents, and poor ageing parents could not afford to take care of their adult children if they fell upon hard times (Ruggles 2003).
5 MacDonald with Storkey and Raab, 2001: 22, table 3.6.
6 Phillipson and his colleagues have speculated that older women may still act as what they call 'neighbourhood keepers', 'vigilant about the changing fortunes of the localities in which they have invested' (Phillipson et al. 1999: 741).
7 M. Kuhn, cited in the preface of Phillipson and Walker 1986: p. xiii.

Chapter 8 Fog-lamps and Leitmotifs

1 As Marwick has pointed out, many of those who sought to articulate and engineer the 'generational' rupture with the cultures of cautious content that seemed to dominate the immediate post-war period were actually born in the decades before the war (Marwick 1998: 67).
2 Interview transcript reported in Gunn and Bell 2002: 115.

3 Apart from anything else, money had to be earned, whereas in Modernity 2 progressively larger amounts of credit are made available through credit cards whose main function is to encourage spending; see Manning 2002.

4 See Allen and Bewley 1935: 5, table, and 32–3, table A, first column.

5 Office of National Statistics 2002a: 17, table 1.2.

6 This is not to imply that we are unaware of the ideological nature of choice; see Žižek 2001: 116–18.

7 Authors' own analyses of the 2001 Living in Britain General Household Survey data archive (University of Essex).

8 See National Endowment for the Arts 1994, 1995, 1999.

9 This shift in responsibility does not mean that the state no longer wishes to play a central role in insuring systems of old age poverty relief. However, the retrenchments that are being made do result in a retraction of responsibility for insuring effective income replacement in retirement and transferring risk to the individual (see Bonoli 1999).

10 This phrase of Bauman's (1991: 2) refers to the increasing capacity of capital to reproduce and expand itself beyond the productivity of labour, in areas such as futures, derivatives and various forms of financial spread betting.

11 We are referring to the 'globalization thesis' that some consider progressively threatens to undermine the power of the nation-state to guarantee anything beyond the barest of social rights to its citizens. See Ohmae (1996), for a strong version of this thesis, and Hirst and Thompson (1999) for a weak version. The terms 'strong' and 'weak', we should hasten to add, are those employed by Linda Weiss, in her critique of this thesis (Weiss 1997).

12 Typical of this genre are the European Commission's 1994 paper on growth and national competitiveness and the European Employers' Federation's 1998 report on Europe's competitiveness (UNICE 1998).

13 See AARP website: <www.aarp.org/prescriptiondrugs/informed/articles/a2003-11-20-position.html>, accessed 28 Jan. 2004.

References

Abrams, M. 1951: *Social Surveys and Social Action*. Heinemann, London.

Abrams, M., Rose, R. and Hinden, M. 1960: *Must Labour Lose?* Penguin Books, Harmondsworth.

Abrams, P. 1970: Rites de passage: the conflict of generations in industrial society. *Journal of Contemporary History*, 5, 175–90.

Ackers, L. and Dwyer, P. 2004: Fixed laws, fluid lives: the citizenship status of post-retirement migrants in the European Union. *Ageing & Society*, 24, 451–75.

Akhtar, M. and Humphries, S. 2001: *The Fifties and Sixties: A Lifestyle Revolution*. Boxtree, London.

Allen, R. G. D. and Bewley, A. L. 1935: *Family Expenditure: A Study of its Variation*. PS King & Son, London.

Althusser, L. 1969: *For Marx*. Allen Lane, London.

Althusser, L. 1971: *Lenin and Philosophy and Other Essays*. New Left Books, London.

American Association of Retired Persons (AARP) 2004: <www.aarp.org/prescriptiondrugs/informed/articles/a2003-11-20-position.html>, accessed 28 Jan. 2004.

Anderson, B. 1991: *Imagined Communities*. Verso, London.

Anderson, M. 1985: The emergence of the modern life cycle in Britain. *Social History*, 10, 69–87.

Arber, S. and Ginn, J. 1991: The invisibility of age: gender and class in later life. *Sociological Review*, 39, 260–91.

Arber, S. and Ginn, J. 1995: Connecting gender and ageing: a new beginning. In S. Arber and J. Ginn (eds), *Connecting Gender and Ageing*, Open University Press, Buckingham, 173–8.

Ardagh, J. 1970: *The New French Revolution*. Penguin Books, Harmondsworth.

Atkinson, R. and Kintrea, K. 2001: Disentangling area effects: evidence from deprived and non-deprived neighbourhoods. *Urban Studies*, 38, 2277–98.

Baemreither, J. M. 1889: *English Associations of Working Men*. Swan Sonnenschein, London.

Bagnell, G. 1996: Consuming the past. In S. Edgell, K. Heatherington and A. Warde (eds), *Consumption Matters*, Blackwell, Oxford, 227–47.

Balfour, J. L. and Kaplan, G. A. 2002: Neighbourhood environment and loss of physical function in older adults: evidence from the Alameda County study. *American Journal of Epidemiology*, 155, 507–15.

Barnes, C. and Oliver, M. 1995: *Disability Rights: Rhetoric and Reality in the UK*. Macmillan, London.

Barrett, A. E. 2003: Socioeconomic status and age identity: the role of dimensions of health in the subjective construction of age. *Journal of Gerontology*, 58B, S101–9.

Barrett, M. 1980: *Women's Oppression Today: Problems in Marxist Feminist Analysis*. Verso, London.

Bateman, H., Kingston, G. and Piggott, J. 2001: *Forced Saving: Mandating Private Retirement Incomes*. Cambridge University Press, Cambridge.

Bauman, Z. 1991: *Intimations of Postmodernity*. Routledge, London.

Bauman, Z. 1998: *Work, Consumerism and the New Poor*. Open University Press, Buckingham.

Bauman, Z. 2000: *Globalization: The Human Consequences*. Polity, Cambridge.

Bauman, Z. 2001: *The Individualized Society*. Polity, Cambridge.

Bawin-Legros, B. and Stassen, J.-F. 2002: Inter-generational solidarity: between the family and the state. *Current Sociology*, 50, 243–62.

Beck, U. 1990: *Risk Society*. Sage, London.

Beck, U. 2000: *The Brave New World of Work*. Polity, Cambridge.

Beck, U. and Beck-Gernsheim, E. 2001: *Individualization*. Sage, London.

Beck, U., Bonss, W. and Lau, C. 2003: The theory of reflexive modernisation: problematic, hypotheses and research programme. *Theory, Culture & Society*, 20, 1–33.

Beck-Gernsheim, E. 2002: *Reinventing the Family: In Search of New Lifestyles*. Polity, Cambridge.

Becker, H. A. 1991: A pattern of generations and its consequences. In H. A. Becker, *Dynamics of Cohort and Generations Research*, Thesis Publishers, Amsterdam, 201–25.

Becker, H. A. 2000: Discontinuous change and generational contracts. In S. Arber and C. Attias-Donfuit (eds), *The Myth of Generational Conflict: The Family and the State in Ageing Societies*, Routledge, London, 114–32.

Beldon, Russonello and Stewart 2001: *In the Middle: A Report on Multi-cultural Boomers Coping with Family and Aging Issues*. AARP, Washington, DC.

Bell, C. and Newby, H. 1971: *Community Studies*. George Allen & Unwin Ltd., London.

Benson, J. 1989: *The Working Class in Britain, 1850–1939*. Longman, London.

Benson, J. 1994: *The Rise of Consumer Society in Britain, 1880–1980*. Longman, London.

Bergman, W. 1992: The problem of time in sociology: an overview of the literature on the state of theory and research on the 'sociology of time', 1900–82. *Time & Society*, 1, 81–134.

Bewley, A. L. 1937: *Wages and Income in the United Kingdom since 1860*. Cambridge University Press, Cambridge.

Binstock, R. 2000: Older people and voting participation: past and future. *The Gerontologist*, 40, 18–31.

Blackburn, R. 2002: *Banking on Death or Investing in Life: The History and Future of Pensions*. Verso, London.

Bonoli, G. 1999: Globalisation, the Welfare State and Recommodification, unpublished paper, Dept. of Social and Policy Sciences, University of Bath.

Bookchin, M. 1997: *From Urbanization to Cities*. Cassel, London.

Booker, C. 1970: *The Neophiliacs: Revolution in English Life in the Fifties and Sixties*. Fontana, London.

Bourdieu, P. 1997: *Outline of a Theory of Practice*. Cambridge University Press, Cambridge.

Bourdieu, P. 1992: *Distinction: A Social Critique of the Judgement of Taste*. Routledge, London.

Bourdieu, P. and Wacquant, L. J. D. 1996: *An Invitation to Reflexive Sociology*. Polity, Cambridge.

Bourke, J. 1994: *Working Class Cultures in Britain, 1890–1960: Gender, Class and Ethnicity*. Routledge, London.

Bourne, R. S. 1911: The two generations. In R. D. Thau and J. S. Heflin (eds), *Generations Apart: Xers vs. Boomers vs. the Elderly*, Prometheus Books, Amherst, NY, 1997, 95–109.

Bowden, S. and Offner, A. 1996: The technological revolution that never was. In V. de Grazia and E. Furlough (eds), *The Sex of Things: Gender and Consumption in Historical Perspective*, University of California Press, Berkeley, 212–43.

Brenner, R. 2004: A new boom or a new bubble? *New Left Review*, ser. 2, 25, 57–102.

Brooks, R., Regan, S. and Robinson, P. 2002: *A New Contract for Retirement*. IPPR, Bristol.

Brundage, A. 2002: *The English Poor Laws, 1700–1930*. Palgrave, Basingstoke.

Bulmer, M. 1985: The rejuvenation of community studies? Neighbours networks and policy. *Sociological Review*, 33, 430–48.

Burkhauser, R. V. and Poupore, J. G. 1997: A cross-national comparison of permanent inequality in the United States and Germany. *Review of Economics and Statistics*, 79, 10–17.

Bury, M. 1995: Ageing, gender and sociological theory. In S. Arber and J. Ginn (eds), *Connecting Gender and Ageing*, Open University Press, Buckingham, 15–29.

Calhoun, C. 1980: Community: toward a variable conceptualization for comparative research. *Social History*, 5, 105–29.

Calhoun, C. 1998: Community without propinquity revisited: communications technology revisited and the transformation of the urban public space. *Sociological Inquiry*, 68, 373–97.

Campbell, Jane 2003: Choose life. *The Guardian*, Aug. 26.

Cantor, M. H. 1975: Life space and the social support systems of the inner city elderly. *The Gerontologist*, 15, 23–7.

Capuzzo, P. 2001: Youth culture and consumption in contemporary Europe. *Contemporary European History*, 10, 155–70.

Carter, S. B. and Sutch, R. 1996: Myth of the industrial scrap heap: a revisionist view of turn of the century American retirement. *Journal of Economic History*, 56, 5–38.

Casey, B. and Yamada, A. 2002: Getting older, getting poorer? A study of the earnings, pensions assets and living arrangements of older people in nine countries. *Labour Market and Social Policy Occasional Papers*, no. 60. OECD, Paris.

Castells, M. 1997: *The Power of Identity*. Blackwell, Oxford.

Chan, S. and Stevens, A. H. 2003: What you don't know can't help you: pension knowledge and retirement decision making. *NBER Working Paper 10185*. NBER, Cambridge, Mass.

Chiarini, B. 1999: The composition of union membership: the role of pensioners in Italy. *British Journal of Industrial Relations*, 37, 577–600.

Clark, G. 2003: Pension security in the global economy: markets and national institutions in the 21st century. *Environment and Planning A*, 35, 1339–56.

Clark, R. and Bewley, A. 1936: *Family Expenditure: A Study of its Variation*. P.S. King & Son, London.

Classen, S. 1997: Southern discomforts: the racial struggle over popular TV. In L. Spigel and M. Curtin (eds), *The Revolution wasn't Televised:*

Sixties Television and Social Conflict, Routledge, New York, 305–26.

Cohen, A. P. 1989: *The Symbolic Construction of Community*. Routledge, London.

Cohen, L. 2003: *A Consumers' Republic: The Politics of Mass Consumption in PostWar America*. Alfred A. Knopf, New York.

Cohen, W. J. 1958: Income maintenance and medical insurance. In E. W. Burgess (ed.), *Aging in Western Culture*, University of Chicago Press, Chicago, 76–105.

Collins, C. A., Estes, C. L. and Bradshaw, J. E. 2001: Inequality and aging: the creation of dependency. In C. L. Estes and Associates (eds), *Social Policy & Aging*, Sage, London, 137–63.

Collins, D. and Tisdell, C. 2000: Changing travel patterns with age: Australian evidence and the need to modify current theories. *Australian Journal of Hospitality Management*, 7, 15–25.

Collins, D. and Tisdell, C. 2002: Age-related lifecycles: purpose variations. *Annals of Tourism Research*, 29, 801–18.

Comer, C. A. P. 1911: A letter to the rising generation. In R. D. Thau and J. S. Heflin (eds), *Generations Apart: Xers vs. Boomers vs. the Elderly*, Prometheus Books, Amherst, NY, 1997, 81–94.

Conrad, C. 1990: La Naissance de la retraite moderne: l'Allemagne dans une comparaison internationale (1850–1960). *Population*, 3, 531–63.

Conseil d'Orientation des Retraites 2001: *Retraites: renouveler le contrat social entre les génération*. Paris.

Corsten, M. 1999: The time of generations. *Time & Society*, 8, 249–72.

Costa, D. L. 1998: *The Evolution of Retirement*. University of Chicago Press, Chicago.

Crompton, R. 1996: Gender and class analysis. In D. J. Lee and B. S. Turner (eds), *Conflicts about Class: Debating Inequality in Late Industrialisation*, Longman, London, 115–26.

Cross, G. 2000: *An All-Consuming Century: Why Commercialism Won in Modern America*. Columbia University Press, New York.

Crouch, C. 1999: *Social Change in Western Europe*. Oxford University Press, Oxford.

Crow, G. 2000: Developing sociological arguments through community studies. *International Journal of Social Research Methodology: Theory and Practice*, 3, 173–87.

Crow, G. P. and Allan, G. 1995: Community types, community typologies and community time. *Time & Society*, 4, 147–66.

Cutler, N. 1977: Political socialization research as generational analysis: the cohort approach versus the lineage approach. In S. A. Renshon (ed.), *Handbook of Political Socialization*, Free Press, New York, 294–326.

Davidson, C. 1982: *A Woman's Work is Never Done: A History of Housework in the British Isles, 1650–1950*. Chatto and Windus, London.

Deller, S. C. 1995: Economic impact of retirement migration. *Economic Development Quarterly*, 9, 25–38.

Department of Employment 1986: *Family Expenditure Survey, 1984/5*. HMSO, London.

Department of Work and Pensions, Pensions Analysts Division 2003: *The Pensioners' Income Series, 2001/2*. The Stationery Office, London.

Devine, F. 1992: *Affluent Workers Revisited: Privatism and the Working Class*. Edinburgh University Press, Edinburgh.

De Vos, S. and Arias, E. 2003: A note on the living arrangements of elders, 1970–2000 with special emphasis on Hispanic subgroup differentials. *Population Research and Policy Review*, 22, 91–101.

Diebolt, C. and Reimat, A. 1997: Old age policies in France and Germany from the last decades of the nineteenth century to the First World War: a quantitative redefinition. *Historical Social Research*, 22, 181–97.

DiPrete, T. A. and MacManus, P. A. 2000: Family change, employment transitions and the welfare state: household income dynamics in the United States and Germany. *American Sociological Review*, 65, 343–70.

DiPrete, T. A., de Graaf, P., Luijkx, R., Tahlin, M. and Blossfeld, H.-P. 1997: Collectivist versus individualist mobility regimes? How welfare state and labor market structure condition the mobility effects of structural change in four countries. *American Journal of Sociology*, 103, 318–58.

Disney, R. and Whitehouse, E. 2001: Cross-country comparisons of pensioners' incomes. *Dept of Social Security Research Report No. 142*. HMSO, London.

Dreyfus, M. 1996: The labour movement and mutual benefit societies: towards an international approach. In M. van der Linder (ed.), *Social Security Mutualism: The Comparative History of Mutual Benefit Societies*, Peter Lang AG, Berne, 673–84.

Dumenil, L. 1995: *Modern Temper: American Culture and Society in the 1920s*. Hill and Wang, New York.

Edmunds, J. and Turner, B. 2002: *Generational Consciousness: Narrative and Politics*. Rowman and Littlefield, Lanham, Md.

Ekerdt, D., Dingel, M., Bowen, M. and Sergeant, J. 2003: Managing and disposing of possessions in later life. *The Gerontologist*, 43, special issue 1, 257.

Engelen, E. 2003: The logic of funding European pension restructuring and the dangers of financialisation. *Environment and Planning A*, 35, 1357–72.

Erickson, R. and Goldthorpe, J. 1993: *The Constant Flux*. Clarendon Press, Oxford.

Esping-Andersen, G. 1990: *The Three Worlds of Welfare Capitalism*. Princeton University Press, Princeton, NJ.

Esping-Andersen, G. 2000: Two societies, one sociology and no theory. *British Journal of Sociology*, 51, 59–77.

Etzioni, A. 1996: *The New Golden Rule: Community and Morality in a Democratic Society*. Basic Books, New York.

European Union 1994: *Growth, Competitiveness and Employment*. European Union, Brussels.

Evers, A. and Wolf, J. 1999: Political organisation and participation of older people: traditions and changes in five European countries. In A. Walker and G. Nagele (eds), *The Politics of Old Age in Europe*, Open University Press, Buckingham, 42–61.

Ewen, S. 1976: *Captains of Consciousness: Advertising and the Social Roots of the Consumer Culture*. McGraw Hill Book Co., New York.

Fass, P. S. 1979: *The Damned and the Beautiful: American Youth in the 1920s*. Oxford University Press, New York.

Ferguson N. 2004: *Colossus: The Rise and Fall of the American Empire*. Allen Lane, London.

Fogel, R. W. 2003: Changes in the process of aging during the twentieth century: findings and procedures of the early indicators project. *NBER Working Paper 9941*. NBER, Cambridge, Mass.

Fokkema, T., Gierveld, J. and Nijkamp, P. 1996: Big cities, big problems: reason for the elderly to move? *Urban Studies*, 33, 353–77.

Frankenberg, R. 1966: *Communities in Britain*. Penguin Books, Harmondsworth.

Fraser, N. 1995: From redistribution to recognition? Dilemmas of justice in a post socialist age. *New Left Review*, 212, 68–93.

Fraser, N. 1997: *Justice Interruptus*. Routledge, New York.

Fukuyama, F. 1996: *Trust: The Social Virtues and the Creation of Prosperity*. Penguin Books, Harmondsworth.

Fukuyama, F. 1999: *The Great Disruption: Human Nature and the Reconstitution of Social Order*. Profile Books, London.

Gallie, D. 2000: The labour force. In A. H. Halsey (ed.), *Twentieth Century British Social Trends*, Macmillan Press, London, 281–323.

Ghilarducci, T. 1992: *Labour's Capital: The Economics and Politics of Private Pensions*. MIT Press, Cambridge, Mass.

Giddens, A. 1991: *Modernity and Self-Identity: Self and Society in the Late Modern Age*. Polity, Cambridge.

Giddens, A. 2000: *The Third Way and its Critics*. Polity, Cambridge.

Gilleard, C. and Higgs, P. 2000: *Cultures of Ageing: Self, Citizen and the Body*. Prentice-Hall, Harlow.

Gilleard, C. and Higgs, P. 2002: The Third Age: class, cohort or generation. *Ageing & Society*, 22, 369–82.

Glass, R. 1966: Conflict in cities. In A. V. S. de Reuck and Julie Knight (eds), *Ciba Foundation Symposium on Conflict in Society*, J. & A. Churchill, London, 82–103.

Goldthorpe, J. H., Lockwood, D., Bechhofer, E. and Platt, J. 1968: *The Affluent Worker: Industrial Attitudes and Behaviour*. Cambridge University Press, Cambridge.

Goldthorpe, J. H., Lockwood, D., Bechhofer, E. and Platt, J. 1969: *The Affluent Worker in the Class Structure*. Cambridge University Press, Cambridge.

Goodman, A., Mick, M. and Shephard, A. 2003: *Sharing in the Nation's Prosperity? Pensioner Poverty in Britain*. Institute for Fiscal Studies, London.

Graebner, W. 1980: *A History of Retirement*. Yale University Press, New Haven.

Gramsci, A. 1957: *The Modern Prince and Other Writings*. Lawrence & Wishart, London.

Gratton, B. 1996: The poverty of impoverishment theory: the economic well-being of the elderly, 1890–1950. *Journal of Economic History*, 56, 39–61.

Gray, J. 1997: *Endgames: Questions in Late Modern Political Thought*. Polity, Cambridge.

Green-Pedersen, C. and Haverland, M. 2002: The new politics and scholarship of the welfare state. *Journal of European Social Policy*, 12, 43–51.

Grossberg, L. 1996: Identity and Cultural Studies: is that all there is? In S. Hall and P. du Gay (eds), *Questions of Cultural Identity*, Sage Publications, London, 87–107.

Guillemin, O. and Roux, V. 2003: The living standards of French households between 1970 and 1999. In *Données Sociales: La Société Française, 2002–3*, INSEE, Paris, 1–12.

Gunn, S. and Bell, R. 2002: *Middle Classes: Their Rise and Sprawl*. Cassell & Co., London.

Gustafson, P. 2001: Retirement migration and transnational lifestyles. *Ageing & Society*, 21, 371–94.

Haas, W. H. and Serow, W. J. 2002: The baby boom, amenily retirement migration and retirement communities: will the golden age of retirement continue? *Research on Aging*, 24, 150–64.

Habermas, J. 1988: *Legitimation Crisis*. Blackwell, Oxford.

Hakim, C. 1979: *Occupational Segregation*. Department of Employment Research Publication, no. 9. HMSO, London.

Hakim, C. 2000: *Work – Lifestyle Choices in the Twenty First Century: Preference Theory*. Oxford University Press, Oxford.

Halter, M. 2000: *Shopping for Identity: The Marketing of Ethnicity*. Schocken, New York.

Han, S. K. and Moen, P. 1999: Clocking out: temporal patterning of retirement. *American Journal of Sociology*, 105, 191–236.

Hancock, R., Askham, J., Nelson, H. and Tinker, A. 1999: *Home Ownership in Later Life: Financial Benefit or Burden?* Joseph Rowntree Foundation, York Publishing Services, York.

Hannah, L. 1985: Why employer based pension plans? The case of Britain. *Journal of Economic History*, 45, 347–54.

Hannah, L. 1986: *Inventing Retirement: Development of Occupational Pensions in Britain*. Cambridge University Press, Cambridge.

Hardy, M. A. and Waite, L. 1997: Doing time: reconciling biography with history in the study of social change. In M. A. Hardy (ed.), *Studying Aging and Social Change*, Sage Publications, London, 1–21.

Harris, N. 2003: *The Return of Cosmopolitan Capital: Globalization, the State and War*. Palgrave, Basingstoke.

Harvey, D. 1989: *The Condition of Postmodernity*. Blackwell, Oxford.

Haseler, S. 2000: *The Super Rich: The Unjust New World of Global Capitalism*. Macmillan, London.

Hay, C. and Marsh, D. 2000: Introduction. In C. Hay and D. Marsh (eds), *Demystifying Globalization*, Palgrave, London, 1–17.

Heath, A., Jowell, R. and Curtis, J. 1985: *How Britain Votes*. Pergamon, Oxford.

Hebdige, D. 1979: *Subculture: The Meaning of Style*. Methuen, London.

Hill, J. 2002: *Sport, Leisure and Culture in Twentieth Century Britain*. Palgrave, London.

Hine, T. 2000: *The Rise and Fall of the American Teenager*. HarperCollins, New York.

Hirshbein, L. D. 2001: The flapper and the fogey: representations of gender and age in the 1920's. *Journal of Family History*, 26, 112–37.

Hirst, P. and Thompson, G. 1999: *Globalization in Question*. Polity, Cambridge.

Hobsbawm, E. 1989: *Politics for a Rational Left*. Verso, London.

Hobson, D. 1999: *The National Wealth: Who Gets What in Britain*. HarperCollins, London.

Hodge, G. 1991: The economic impact of retirees on smaller communities. *Research on Aging*, 13, 39–54.

Hope, J. and Havir, L. 2002: You bet they're having fun! Older Americans and casino gambling. *Journal of Aging Studies*, 16, 177–97.

Huber, E. and Stephens, J. 2001: *Development and Crisis of the Welfare*

State: Parties and Policies in Global Markets. University of Chicago Press, Chicago.

Hudson, R. 1999: The evolution of the welfare state: shifting rights and responsibilities for the old. In M. Minkler and C. Estes (eds), *Critical Gerontology: Perspectives from Political and Moral Economy*, Baywood, Amityville, NY, 329–44.

Iceland, J. 2003: *Poverty in America, A Handbook.* University of California Press, Berkeley.

Inglehart, R. 1997: *Modernization and Postmodernization: Cultural, Economic and Political Change in 43 Societies.* Princeton University Press, Princeton, NJ.

Inland Revenue 2003: <www.inlandrevenue.gov.uk/stats/personal_wealth/dopw_t02_1mf.htm>, accessed 26 Oct. 2003.

Jameson, F. 1984: Postmodernism or the cultural logic of late capitalism. *New Left Review,* 146, 53–92.

Johnson, P. 1994: The employment and retirement of older men in England and Wales, 1881–1981. *Economic History Review,* 47, 106–28.

Johnson, P. and Stears, G. 1995: Pensioner income inequality. *Fiscal Studies,* 16, 69–93.

Kammen, M. 1999: *American Culture, American Tastes.* Basic Books, New York.

Keegan, C., Gross, S., Fisher, L. and Remez, S. 2002: *Boomers at Midlife: The AARP Life Stage Study.* AARP, Washington, DC.

Keister, L. A. 2000: *Wealth in America: Trends in Wealth Inequality.* Cambridge University Press, New York.

Kertzer, D. I. 1983: Generation as a sociological problem. *Annual Review of Sociology,* 9, 125–49.

King, R., Warnes, A. M. and Williams, A. M. 1998: International retirement migration in Europe. *International Journal of Population Geography,* 4, 91–111.

Kingston, P. W. 2000: *The Classless Society.* Stanford University Press, Stanford, Calif.

Kirkwood, T. 1999: *Time of our Lives: The Science of Aging.* Oxford University Press, Oxford.

Klein, J. 2003: *For All These Rights: Business, Labor and the Shaping of America's Public–Private Welfare State.* Princeton University Press, Princeton, NJ.

Kohli, M. 1996: *The Problem of Generations: Family, Economics, Politics.* Public Lecture no. 14. Institute for Advanced Studies, Collegium Budapest.

Kohli, M. 1999: Private and public transfers between generations: linking the family and the state. *European Societies,* 1, 81–104.

Kohli, M. and Rein, M. 1991: The changing balance of work and retirement. In M. Kohli, M. Rein, A.-M. Guillemard and H. van Gunsteren (eds), *Time for Retirement: Comparative Studies of Early Exit from the Labor Force*, Cambridge University Press, Cambridge, 1–35.

Krueger, P. M., Rogers, R. G., Hummer, R. A., LeClere, F. B. and Bond Huie, S. A. 2003: Socioeconomic status and age: the effect of income sources and portfolios on US adult mortality. *Sociological Forum*, 18, 465–82.

Lane, J. E. and Ersson, S. O. 1999: *Politics and Society in Western Europe*. Sage, London.

Lasch, C. 1980: *The Culture of Narcissism*. Abacus, London.

Lash, S. and Urry, J. 1987: *The End of Organized Capitalism*. Polity, Cambridge.

Laslett, P. 1983: One-class society. In R. S. Neale (ed.), *History and Class: Essential Readings in Theory and Interpretation*, Blackwell, Oxford, 196–221.

Laslett, P. 1989: *A Fresh Map of Life*. Weidenfield & Nicolson, London.

Lee, C. 2002: Sectoral shift and labor force participation of older males in the United States, 1880–1940. *Journal of Economic History*, 62, 512–23.

Lee, C. 2003: Labor market status of older males in the United States, 1880–1940. *NBER Working Paper, 9550*. NBER, Cambridge, Mass.

Lee, D. J. and Turner, B. S. (eds) 1996: *Conflicts about Class: Debating Equality in Late Industrialism*. Longman, London.

Le Gall, D. and Martin, C. 1997: Fashioning a new family tie: stepparents and step-grandchildren. In M. Gullestad and M. Segalen (eds), *Family and Kinship in Europe*, Pinter, London, 183–201.

Leisering, L. and Liebfried, S. 1999: *Time and Poverty in Western Welfare States*. Cambridge University Press, Cambridge.

Levy, F. 1987: *Dollars and Dreams: The Changing American Income Distribution*. Sage Publications, New York.

Lewis, G. 2000: *'Race', Gender, Social Welfare: Encounters in a Postcolonial Society*. Polity, Cambridge.

Little, D. 2000: *Forty Years of Coronation Street*. Granada, London.

Lockwood, D. 1966: Sources of variation in working class images of society. *Sociological Review*, 14, 249–67.

Longhurst, B. and Savage, M. 1996: Social class, consumption and the influence of Bourdieu: some critical issues. In S. Edgell, K. Heatherington and A. Warde (eds), *Consumption Matters*, Blackwell, Oxford, 274–301.

Longino, C. F., Perzynski, A. T. and Stoller, E. P. 2002: Pandora's briefcase: unpacking the retirement migration decision. *Research on Aging*, 24, 29–49.

Luckett, M. 1997: Girl watchers: Patty Duke and teen TV. In L. Spigel and M. Curtin (eds), *The Revolution wasn't Televised: Sixties Television and Social Conflict*, Routledge, New York, 95–116.

Lupton, D. 1995: *The Imperative of Health: Public Health and the Regulated Body*. Sage, London.

Lynes, T. 1986: *Paying for Pensions: The French Experience*, Suntory–Toyota International Centre for Economics, London School of Economics, London.

MacDonald, C. with Storkey, H. and Raab, G. 2001: *Older People in Scotland: Results from the First Year of the Scottish Household Survey*. Scottish Executive Central Research Unit, Edinburgh.

Macdonald, Dwight 1958: A caste, a culture, a market. *The New Yorker*, Nov.

Macfarlane, A. 1977: History, anthropology and the study of communities. *Social History*, 5, 631–52.

Macnicol, J. and Blaikie, A. 1989: The politics of retirement 1908–1948. In M. Jefferys (ed.), *Growing Old in the Twentieth Century*, Routledge, London, 21–42.

Maffesoli, M. 1996: *The Time of the Tribes*. Sage, London.

Malik, K. 1996: *The Meaning of Race*. Macmillan, London.

Mannheim, K. 1952/1997: The problem of generations. Reproduced in M. A. Hardy (ed.), *Studying Aging and Social Change*, Sage Publications, London, 22–65.

Mannheim, K. 1960: *Ideology and Utopia: An Introduction to the Sociology of Knowledge*. Routledge, Kegan and Paul, London.

Manning, R. 2002: *Credit Card Nation: The Consequences of America's Addiction to Credit*. Basic Books, New York.

Manton, K. G. and Gu, X. 2001: Changes in the prevalence of chronic disability in the United States black and nonblack population above age 65 from 1982 to 1999. *Proceedings of the National Academy of Science*, 98, 6354–9.

Marcuse, H. 1964: *One-Dimensional Man*. Routledge, London.

Marks, D. 1999: *Disability: Controversial Debates and Psychosocial Perspectives*. Routledge, London.

Marshall, T. H. 1950/1992: *Citizenship and Social Class*. Pluto Press, London, 1st published 1950.

Marsh, D. C. 1965: *The Changing Social Structure of England and Wales, 1871–1961*. Routledge and Kegan Paul, London.

Marwick, A. 1998: *The Sixties*. Oxford University Press, Oxford.

Mason, K. O., Winsborough, H. H., Mason, W. M. and Poole, W. K.

1973: Some methodological issues in cohort analysis of archival data. *American Sociological Review*, 38, 242–58.

Matelski, M. J. 1999: *Soap Operas Worldwide: Cultural and Serial Realities*. McFarland & Co., Jefferson, NC.

Mayer, K. U. and Schoplin, U. 1989: The state and the lifecourse. *Annual Review of Sociology*, 15, 187–209.

McGarry, K. and Schoeni, R. F. 2000: Social security, economic growth and the rise in elderly widows' independence in the twentieth century. *Demography*, 37, 221–36.

McIntosh, M. 1996: Feminism and social policy. In D. Taylor (ed.), *Critical Social Policy: A Reader*, Sage, London, 13–26.

Messinger, S. L. 1955: Organisational transformation: a case study of a declining social movement. *American Sociological Review*, 20, 3–10.

Michelon, L. C. 1954: The new leisure class. *American Journal of Sociology*, 59, 371–8.

Middlemas, K. 1979: *Politics in Industrial Society*. André Deutsch, London.

Millar, R. 1966: *The New Classes*. Longmans, Green & Co., London.

Mings, R. C. 1997: Tracking 'snowbirds' in Australia: winter sun seekers in far north Queensland. *Australian Geographical Studies*, 35, 168–82.

Ministry of Labour and National Service 1957: *Report of an Enquiry into Household Expenditure, 1953–54*. HMSO, London.

Minns, S. 2000: *The Cold War against Welfare*. Verso, London.

Mishra, R. 1984: *The Welfare State in Crisis*. Wheatsheaf Books, Hemel Hempstead.

Mitchell, D. J. B. 2000: *Pensions, Politics and the Elderly: Historic Social Movements and their Lessons for our Aging Society*. M. E. Sharpe, Armont, NY.

Moehling, C. 2001: Women's work and men's unemployment. *Journal of Economic History*, 61, 926–49.

Morris, C. R. 1997: *The AARP*. Times Books, New York.

Mukherjee, R. 1952: A study of social mobility between three generations. In D. V. Glass (ed.), *Social Mobility in Britain*, Routledge & Kegan Paul, London, 266–90.

Mullard, M. 1993: *The Politics of Public Expenditure*. Routledge, London.

Munroe, W. B. 1926: *The Government of American Cities*. Macmillan, New York.

Murdock, G. and McCron, R. 1976: Consciousness of class and consciousness of generation. In S. Hall, J. Clarke, T. Jefferson and B. Roberts (eds), *Resistance through Rituals*, Hutchinson, London, 192–207.

Myles, J. 2002: A new social contract for the elderly? In G. Esping-

Andersen (ed.), *Why We Need a New Welfare State*, Oxford, Oxford University Press, 130–72.

Nasow, D. 1999: *Going Out: The Rise and Fall of Public Amusements*. Harvard University Press, Cambridge, Mass.

National Endowment for the Arts 1994: *Demographic Differences in Arts Attendance: 1982–1992*. Research Division Note #51, NEA, Washington, DC.

National Endowment for the Arts 1995: *Age and Arts Participation: With a Focus on the Baby Boom Generation*. NEA, Washington, DC.

National Endowment for the Arts 1999: *1997 Survey of Public Participation in the Arts: Summary Report*. NEA, Washington, DC.

Newbold, K. B. 1995: *Determinants of Elderly Interstate Migration in the US: 1985–1990*. Department of Geography, University of Illinois, Urbana, Ill.

Nield, Lt. Col. J. C. 1898: *Report on Old Age Pensions, Charitable Relief and State Insurance*. Government Printers, Sydney, New South Wales.

Nisbet, R. A. 1970: *The Sociological Tradition*. Heinemann, London.

O'Connor, J. 1987: *The Meaning of Crisis*. Blackwell, Oxford.

O'Donnell, H. 1998: *Good Times, Bad Times: Soap Operas and Society in Western Europe*. Leicester University Press, London.

Office of National Statistics 2002a: *Family Spending: A Report on the 2000–2001 Family Expenditure Survey*. The Stationery Office, London.

Office of National Statistics 2002b: *Living in Britain, Results from the 2000 General Household Survey*. The Stationery Office, London.

Office of National Statistics 2003: *Living in Britain, Results from the 2001 General Household Survey*. The Stationery Office, London.

Office of National Statistics 2004: Time spent on main activity by age group: UK Time Use Survey, <http://www.statistics.gov.uk/statbase>, accessed 12 Jan. 2004.

Office for National Statistics, Pensions Analysts Division 2002: *The Pensioners' Income Series 2000/1*. The Stationery Office, London.

Office for Population and Census Studies 1975a: *General Household Survey, 1972*. HMSO, London.

Office for Population and Census Studies 1975b: *General Household Survey: Supplement Comparing the Housing Situation in France and Great Britain*. HMSO, London.

Office for Population and Census Studies 1978: *General Household Survey, 1975*. HMSO, London.

Office for Population and Census Studies 1982: *General Household Survey, 1980*. HMSO, London.

Office for Population and Census Studies 1987: *General Household Survey, 1985*. HMSO, London.

Office for Population and Census Studies 1992: *General Household Survey, 1990*. HMSO, London.

Office for Population and Census Studies 1997: *General Household Survey, 1995*. HMSO, London.

Oh, J.-H. 2003: Social bonds and the migration intentions of elderly urban residents. *Population Research and Policy Review*, 22, 127–46.

Ohmae, K. 1996: *The End of the Nation State: The Rise of Regional Economies*. Free Press, New York.

Organisation for Economic Co-operation and Development 2001a: *Historical Statistics*. OECD, Paris.

Organisation for Economic Co-operation and Development 2001b: *Ageing and Income: Financial Resources and Retirement in 9 OECD Countries*. OECD, Paris.

Organisation for Economic Co-operation and Development 2002: *OECD Economic Outlook, No. 72, Section V. Increasing Employment: The Role of Later Retirement*. OECD, Paris.

Orloff, A. S. 1993: *The Politics of Pensions: A Comparative Analysis of Britain, Canada and the United States, 1880–1940*. University of Wisconsin Press, Madison.

Ortner, S. 2003: *New Jersey Dreaming: Capital, Culture, and the Class of '58*. Duke University Press, Durham, NC.

Osberg, L. 2001: Poverty among senior citizens: a Canadian success story in international perspective. *Luxembourg Income Study Working Paper No. 274*. Maxwell School of Citizenship and Public Affairs, Syracuse University, New York.

Packard, V. 1957: *The Hidden Persuaders*. Pocket Books, New York.

Pakulski, J. and Waters, M. 1996: *The Death of Class*. Sage Publications, London.

Park, R. E. 1952: *Human Communities: The City and Human Ecology*, vol. 2 of the collected papers of Robert Ezra Park. The Free Press, Glencoe, Ill.

Payne, G. and Roberts, J. 2002: Opening and closing the gates: recent developments in male social mobility in Britain. *Sociological Research Online*, 6, 4 <www.socresonline.org.uk/6/4/payne.html>

Peggs, K. 2000: Which pension? women, risk and pension choice. *Sociological Review*, 48, 349–64.

Perkin, H. 1990: *The Rise of Professional Society: England since 1880*. Routledge, London.

Phillipson, C. 1998: *Reconstructing Old Age*. Sage, London.

Phillipson, C. 2001: History and historical sociology: divergent paths in the study of ageing. *Ageing & Society*, 21, 507–22.

Phillipson, C. and Ahmed, N. 2004: Transnational communities, migration and changing identities in later life: a new research agenda. In S. Daatland and S. Biggs (eds), *Ageing and Diversity: Multiple Pathways and Cultural Migrations*, Policy Press, Bristol, 157–74.

Phillipson, C., Bernard, M., Phillips, J. and Ogg, J. 1999: Older people's experience of community life: patterns of neighbouring in three urban areas. *Sociological Review*, 47, 715–43.

Phillipson, C. and Walker, A. (eds) 1986: *Ageing and Social Policy*. Gower, Aldershot.

Pinol, J.-L. 1993: Occupational and social mobility in Lyon from the late nineteenth to the early twentieth century. In A. Miles and D. Vincent (eds), *Building European Society: Occupational Change and Social Mobility in Europe, 1840–1940*, Manchester University Press, Manchester, 116–39.

Piven, F. F. and Cloward, R. A. 1979: *Poor People's Movements: Why they Succeed, How they Fail*. Vintage, New York.

Piven, F. F. and Cloward, R. A. 1993: *Regulating the Poor: The Functions of Public Welfare*. Vintage, New York.

Polletta, F. and Jasper, J. M. 2001: Collective identity and social movements. *Annual Review of Sociology*, 27, 283–305.

Pomfret, D. M. 2001: Representations of adolescence in the modern city: voluntary provision and work in Nottingham and St Etienne, 1890–1914. *Journal of Family History*, 26, 455–79.

Pooley, C. G. and Turnbull, J. 1998: *Migration and Mobility in Britain since the Eighteenth Century*. UCL Press, London.

Preston, S. H. 1984: Children and the elderly: divergent paths for America's dependents. *Demography*, 21, 435–57.

Pryke, M. and Allen, J. 2000: Monetized time-space: derivatives – money's 'new imaginary'? *Economy & Society*, 29, 264–84.

Putnam, R. 2001: *Bowling Alone*. Simon & Schuster, New York.

Ransom, R. L. and Sutch, R. 1986: The labor of older Americans: retirement of men on and off the job, 1870–1937. *Journal of Economic History*, 46, 1–30.

Reagin, N. 1998: Comparing apples and oranges: housewives and the politics of consumption in interwar Germany. In S. Strasser, C. McGovern and M. Judt (eds), *Getting and Spending: European and American Consumer Societies in the Twentieth Century*, Cambridge University Press, New York/German Historical Institute, Washington, DC, 241–61.

Redfield, R. 1955: *The Little Community*. University of Chicago Press, Chicago.

Rieger, E. and Liebfried, S. 2003: *Limits to Globalization*. Polity, Cambridge.

Ritter, G. A. 1986: *Social Welfare in Germany and Britain.* Berg Publishers, Leamington Spa.

Robert, S. A. and House, J. S. 1996: SES differentials in health by age and alternative indicators of SES. *Journal of Aging and Health,* 8, 359–88.

Roberts, E. 1995: *Women and Families: An Oral History, 1940–1970.* Blackwell, Oxford.

Roberts, K. 2001: *Class in Modern Britain.* Palgrave, London.

Roberts, Y. 2004: Fifty is the new 30 . . . so drop the Zimmer frame jokes. *Observer,* 23 May.

Rodriguez, V., Fernandez-Mayoralas, G. and Rojo, F. 1998: European retirees on the Costa del Sol: a cross-national comparison. *International Journal of Population Geography,* 4, 183–200.

Rogers, A. 1988: Age patterns of elderly migration: an international comparison. *Demography,* 25, 355–70.

Rosenzweig, R. 1983: *Eight Hours for What You Will: Workers and Leisure in an Industrial City.* Cambridge University Press, New York.

Routh, G. 1965: *Occupation and Pay in Great Britain, 1900–1960.* Cambridge University Press, Cambridge.

Rowntree, B. S. 1901: *Poverty: A Study of Town Life.* Macmillan, London.

Rubinstein, R. L. 2002: The Third Age. In R. S. Weiss and S. A. Bass (eds), *Challenges of the Third Age: Meaning and Purpose in Later Life,* Oxford University Press, New York, 29–40.

Ruggles, S. 1987: *Prolonged Connections: The Rise of the Extended Family in Nineteenth Century England and America.* University of Wisconsin Press, Madison.

Ruggles, S. 1993: The transformation of American family structure. *American Historical Review,* 99, 103–28.

Ruggles, S. 2003: Multigenerational families in nineteenth century America. *Continuity & Change,* 18, 139–65.

Ryder, N. B. 1965/1997: The cohort as a concept in the study of social change. Reproduced in M. A. Hardy (ed.), *Studying Aging and Social Change,* Sage Publications, London, 66–92.

Saint-Jours, Y. 1982: France. In P. A. Köhler and H. F. Zacher (eds), *The Evolution of Social Insurance, 1880–1981,* Frances Pinter, London, 93–149.

Savage, M. and Miles, A. 1994: *The Remaking of the British Working Class, 1840–1940.* Routledge, London.

Scambler, G. 2002: *Health and Social Change.* Open University Press, Buckingham.

Scharpf, F. W. 2000: Advanced welfare states in the international economy. *Journal of European Public Policy,* 7, 195–228.

Scholliers, P. (ed.) 1989: *Real Wages in 19ᵗʰ and 20ᵗʰ Century Europe: Historical and Comparative Perspectives*. Berg Publishing, New York.

Scholte, J. A. 2002: Governing global finance. In D. Held and A. McGrew (eds), *Governing Globalization: Power, Authority and Global Governance*, Polity, Cambridge, 189–208.

Schultheis, F. 1997: The missing link: family memory and identity in Germany. In M. Gullestad and M. Segalen (eds), *Family and Kinship in Europe*, Pinter, London, 49–60.

Schuman, H. and Scott, J. 1989: Generations and collective memories. *American Sociological Review*, 54, 359–81.

Seidman, S. 1997: *Difference Troubles: Queering Social Theory and Sexual Politics*. Cambridge University Press, Cambridge.

Silverstein, M. 1995: Stability and change in temporal distance between the elderly and their children. *Demography*, 32, 29–45.

Skocpol, T. 1995: *Social Policy in the United States: Future Possibilities in Historical Perspective*. Princeton University Press, Princeton, NJ.

Slater, D. 1997: *Consumer Culture and Modernity*. Polity, Cambridge.

Smaje, C. 2000: *Natural Hierarchies: The Historical Sociology of Race and Caste*. Blackwell, Oxford.

Smith, T. 2000: *Technology and Capital in the Age of Lean Production*. State University of New York Press, Albany, NY.

Sorensen, A. 2000: Toward a sounder basis for class analysis. *American Journal of Sociology*, 105, 1523–58.

Spigel, L. and Curtin, M. (eds) 1997: *The Revolution wasn't Televised: Sixties Television and Social Conflict*. Routledge, New York.

Spivak, G. C. 1999: *A Critique of Postcolonial Reason: Toward a History of the Vanishing Present*. Harvard University Press, Cambridge, Mass.

Stallmann, J. I. and Espinoza, M. C. 1996: Tourism and retirement migration. *Faculty Paper Series No. FP 97-3*. Dept. of Agricultural Economics, Texas A&M University, College Station, Tex.

Statistics Canada 2003: Average income after tax by economic family types, 1980–2000, <www.statcon.ca/english/Pgdb/famil21a–d>, accessed 11/03/2003.

Stein, M. 1964: *The Eclipse of Community*. Harper & Row, New York.

Stevenson, J. 1984: *British Society, 1914–45*. Penguin Books, Harmondsworth.

Stimpson, R. J., Minnery, J. R., Kabamba, A. and Moon, B. 1996: '*Sun Belt*' *Migration Decisions: A Study of the Gold Coast*. Government Publishing Service, Canberra.

Streib, G. F. 2002: An introduction to retirement communities. *Research on Aging*, 24, 3–9.

Swank, D. 2002: *Global Capital, Political Institutions and Policy: Change in Developed Welfare States.* Cambridge University Press, Cambridge.

Tam, H. 1998: *Communitarianism: A New Agenda for Politics and Citizenship.* Macmillan, London.

Thane, P. 2000: *Old Age in English History: Past Experiences, Present Issues.* Oxford University Press, Oxford.

Thomson, D. 1984: The decline of social welfare: falling state support for the elderly since early Victorian times. *Ageing & Society*, 4, 451–82.

Thomson, D. 1989: The welfare state and generation conflict: winners and losers. In P. Johnson, C. Conrad and D. Thomson (eds), *Workers versus Pensioners: Intergenerational Justice in an Ageing World*, Manchester University Press, Manchester, 33–56.

Thompson, E. P. 1993: *Customs in Common.* The New Press, New York.

Thrift, N. 2000: State sovereignty, globalization and the rise of soft capitalism. In C. Hay and D. Marsh (eds), *Demystifying Globalization*, Palgrave, London, 71–102.

Tönnies, F. 1958: *Gemeinschaft und Gesellschaft* (1886). Trans. as *Community and Association*, ed. C. P. Loomis, Routledge and Kegan Paul, London.

Townsend, P. 1963: *The Family Life of Old People.* Penguin Books, Harmondsworth.

Turner, B. S. 1989: Ageing, politics and sociological theory. *British Journal of Sociology*, 40, 588–606.

Turner, B. S. 1998: Ageing and generational conflict: a reply to Sarah Irwin. *British Journal of Sociology*, 49, 299–304.

UNICE 1998: *Benchmarking Europe's Competitiveness.* European Union, Brussels.

University of Essex: *General Household Survey data archives* (various years). University of Essex.

US Bureau of Labor 2001. *Consumer Expenditure Survey, 1984–1999*, table 3: Average annual expenditure and characteristics: by age of reference person, <www.bls.gov>.

US Census Bureau 1999: *20th Century Statistics.* US Bureau of the Census, Washington, DC.

US Census Bureau 2002: *Housing Vacancies and Homeownership Annual Statistics: 2000*, <www.census.gov/hhes/www/housing/hvs/annual00>, accessed Dec. 2002.

US Census Bureau 2003a: Historical Poverty Tables, table 12, <www.census.gov/hhes/poverty/histpov/hstpov12.html>, accessed 3 Aug. 2003.

US Census Bureau 2003b: Historical Income Tables, <www.census.gov/hhes/income/histic/h10.html>, accessed 3 Aug. 2003.

US Census Bureau 2003c: *Education and Social Stratification Branch, Table A-1*, Internet release date: 21 Mar. 2003.

US Census Bureau 2003d: *Statistical Abstract of the United States: 2002. Section 13. Income, Expenditure and Wealth*. US Bureau of the Census, Washington, DC.

Vallet, L.-A. 1999: Quarante années de mobilité sociale en France: l'évolution de la fluidité sociale a la lumière de modèles récents. *Revue Française de Sociologie*, 40, 5–64.

van Friedeberg, L. 1958: The condition of the West German pensioner before the social reform. In E. W. Burgess (ed.), *Aging in Western Culture*, University of Chicago Press, 457–9.

Veblen, T. 1953: *The Theory of the Leisure Class*. The New American Library, New York, orig. 1899.

Vincent, J. 1999: *Politics, Power and Old Age*. Open University Press, Buckingham.

Vlasblom, J. D. and Nekkers, G. 2001: Regional differences in labour force activity rates of persons aged 55+ within the European Union. *Eurostat Working Papers*, 3/2001/E/no. 6. European Commission, Brussels.

Vogel, J. 2003: The family. *Social Indicators Research*, 64, 393–435.

Vollenwyder, N., Bickel, J.-F., D'Epinay, C. L. and Maystere, C. 2002: The elderly and their families, 1979–94: chatworks and relationships. *Current Sociology*, 50, 263–80.

Wacquant, L. J. D. 1989: Towards a reflexive sociology: a workshop with Pierre Bourdieu. *Sociological Theory*, 7, 26–63.

Wahl, J. 2003: From riches to riches: intergenerational transfers and the evidence from Estate Tax returns. *Social Science Quarterly*, 84, 278–96.

Wahl, H.-W. and Weisman, G. D. 2003: Environmental gerontology at the beginning of the new millennium: reflections on its historical, empirical and theoretical development. *The Gerontologist*, 43, 616–27.

Waidmann, T. and Manton, K. 2000: *Measuring Trends in Disability among the Elderly: An International Review*. Urban Institute, New York.

Wall, R. 2002: Elderly widows and widowers and their co-residents in late 19th and early 20th century England and Wales. *History of the Family*, 7, 139–55.

Wallace, M. 2001: A new approach to neighbourhood renewal in England. *Urban Studies* 38, 2163–6.

Walters, W. H. 2000: Types and patterns of later life migration. *Geografiska Annaler*, 82(B), 129–47.

Walters, W. H. 2002: Later-life migration in the United States: a review of recent research. *Journal of Planning Literature*, 17, 37–66.

Walters, W. H. and Wilder, E. I. 2003: Disciplinary perspectives on later life migration in the core journals of social gerontology. *The Gerontologist*, 43, 758–60.

Warnes, A. M. 1993: The development of retirement migration in Great Britain. *Espace, Populations, Sociétés*, 3, 451–64.

Warnes, A. M. 2001: The international dispersal of pensioners from affluent countries. *International Journal of Population Geography*, 7, 373–88.

Webber, M. M. 1963: Order in diversity: community without propinquity. In L. Wingo (ed.), *Cities and Space*, Johns Hopkins University Press, Baltimore, 29–52.

Weeks, J. 1998: The sexual citizen. *Theory, Culture & Society*, 15, 35–52.

Weeks, J. 2000: *Making Sexual History*. Polity, Cambridge.

Weiss, L. 1997: The myth of the powerless state. *New Left Review*, 225, 3–27.

Weiss, R. S. and Bass, S. A. 2002: Introduction. In R. S. Weiss and S. A. Bass (eds), *Challenges of the Third Age: Meaning and Purpose in Later Life*, Oxford University Press, New York, 3–12.

White, H. C. 1992: Succession and generations: looking back on chains of opportunity. In H. A. Becker (ed.), *Dynamics of Cohort and Generations Research*, Thesis Publishers, Amsterdam, 81–102.

Whitten, P. and Kailis, E. 1999: *Housing Conditions of the Elderly in the EU. Statistics in Focus: Population and Social Conditions*, 3:14/1999, Eurostat, table 3.

Wiedenbeck, R. and den Osgood, R. 1996: *Cases and Materials on Employee Benefits*. West Publishing, St Paul, Minn.

Wilcox, D. F. 1904: *The American City: A Problem in Democracy*, Macmillan, New York.

Williams R. 1983: *Keywords*. Fontana Press, London.

Willmott, P. and Young, M. 1971: *Family and Class in a London Suburb*. New English Library, London.

Woollard, M. 2002: The employment and retirement of older men, 1851–1881: further evidence from the census. *Continuity and Change*, 17, 437–63.

World Bank 1994: *Averting the Old-Age Crisis: Policies to Protect the Old and Promote Growth*. World Bank, Washington, DC.

Wright, E. O. 1997: *Class Counts*. Cambridge University Press, Cambridge.

Yamada, A. 2002: The evolving retirement income package: trends in adequacy and equality in nine OECD countries. *Labour Market and Social Policy Occasional Papers, no. 63*. OECD, Paris.

Young, M. and Willmott, P. 1962 [1957]: *Family and Kinship in East London*. Penguin Books, Harmondsworth.

Zentrum fur Umfragen, Methoden und Analysen Abteilung Soziale

Indikatoren (ZUMA Social Indicators Unit) 2003a: *Social Indicators for Germany: 1950–2001. IV. Income and Income Distribution, 3. Poverty as measured by income.* ZUMA, Mannheim.

Zentrum fur Umfragen, Methoden und Analysen Abteilung Soziale Indikatoren (ZUMA Social Indicators Unit) 2003b: *Social Indicators for Germany: 1950–2001. V. Consumption and Supply,* ZUMA, Mannheim.

Žižek, S. 2001: *On Belief.* Routledge, London.

Zöllner, D. 1982: Germany. In P. A. Köhler and H. F. Zacher (eds), *The Evolution of Social Insurance, 1880–1981,* Frances Pinter, London, 1–92.

Zunz, O. 1998: *Why the American Century?* University of Chicago Press, Chicago.

Zweig, F. 1961: *The Worker in an Affluent Society.* Heinemann, London.

Websites consulted

<www.aarp.org>
<www.corrie.net>
<www.emag.org.uk>
<www.natpencon.org.uk>

Index